Praise for *Money Revolution*

"In addition to exploring philosophical and historical ideas about the role of money in our lives, Shaun M. Rowles also offers a guide to understanding the rapidly changing identity of money. *Money Revolution* is a practical look into our rapidly approaching future for anyone from investor to taxpayer."

Jack Weatherford
New York Times bestselling author of *The History of Money* and *Genghis Khan and the Quest for God*

"An engaging and insightful tour of the phenomenon we know as 'money.' Shaun M. Rowles offers readers a dynamic approach to understanding the rise of cryptocurrency as viewed through the analysis of the evolution of money itself. He reminds us of our role in the longstanding social conversation that seeks to answer 'What is money, and who shall control it?'"

Arthur B. Laffer, PhD
Recipient of the President Medal of Freedom
for contributions in the field of economics

"As the ancient Greek philosopher Heraclitus said, 'The only constant in life is change.' Money is no different. *Money Revolution* shows us that cryptocurrency was born in the same fires of innovation and disruption that in past ages created coins, paper money, and central banks. By tracing the history of money as a series of technological disruptions, Shaun M. Rowles shares why Bitcoin, Ethereum, and other blockchain innovations look as good as gold. This is a must-read book for those who want to understand how disruptions in money, banking, and cryptocurrency force us to change with the times."

Justas Pikelis
Co-founder of Monetha, built on the
Ethereum blockchain; Forbes 30Under30

MONEY
REVOLUTION

MONEY
REVOLUTION

FINTECH DISRUPTION FROM
BULLION TO BITCOIN

SHAUN M. ROWLES

**CONVERSATION
PUBLISHING**

Printed in the United States of America.
First paperback edition October 2021.

10 9 8 7 6 5 4 3 2 1

Cover and layout design by G Sharp Design, LLC.
www.gsharpmajor.com

ISBN 978-1-7359415-6-1 (hardcover)
ISBN 978-1-7359415-7-8 (ebook)

Published by Conversation Publishing.
www.conversationpublishing.com

To my beautiful wife and four amazing children, thank you for your inspiration and eternal confidence! Without your support and encouragement, this book would not have been possible. I could not be more happy and proud to have you in my life.

Follow your passion and you will never work a day in your life.

ACKNOWLEDGMENTS

In a letter to Robert Hooke in 1675, Sir Isaac Newton stated "If I have seen further it is by standing on the shoulders of Giants." The two gentlemen were members of what was originally called "The Royal Society of London for Improving Natural Knowledge," known more commonly as the Royal Society. The Society's motto "Nullius in verba"—taken to mean, "take nobody's word for it"—fosters a sense of the relentless pursuit of knowledge.

The society published Hooke's "Micrographia" and later Newton's "Principia Mathematica," which were breakthrough works that advanced the human understanding of the world around us and set the stage for what scientific advancement was to come. It is no small symbolic gesture that Newton acknowledged those who had come before him while he and his compatriots were busy ushering humanity into a new "system of the world," to borrow the Neal Stephenson phrase.

It is within this context that I offer my own acknowledgement that without the tremendous body of work kindly donated to the human library of knowledge by our predecessors, these pages would be empty. Without the trailblazing of Herodotus of Halicarnassus, we could not claim the legacy of "historian" that we do today. Without Robert Hooke, we would not see the world from its smallest vantage, and without Sir Isaac Newton and Gottfried Wilhelm Leibniz, we may not have progressed with a mathematical understanding of the universe and our place within it.

For the more direct approach to this text, we must first acknowledge the exceptional work of Niall Fergusson. It was Fergusson who opened my eyes to the notion that "Financial history underpins all history" and offered me a valuable platform from which to approach our understanding of monetary society.

Fergusson's work was followed by an equally captivating author, Felix Martin, who took the leap to focus financial history on its main character, Money. In an era of advanced quantitative economic and finance discussions, it was Martin who noted the absence of the role of money itself in these forums. More importantly, it was Martin who most succinctly described the agreement that served as the foundation of central banking and the rationale behind the experiment's 300-year dominance.

Approaching the conversation from an altogether different vantage point, the work of Daniel Kahneman and Amos Tversky paved a path for future behavioral economists Robert Shiller and Dan Ariely to tease out the insights that are helping modernize economic modeling.

These renegades showcased the necessity to refuse to settle. I take to heart this empowering and inspirational quote from Steve Jobs: "Everything around you that you call life was made up by people that were no smarter than you. And you can change it, you can influence it…Once you learn that, you'll never be the same again." In that fashion, I acknowledge the voices that continue to question the system such as James Rickards and G. Edward Griffin.

There are also the scholars who obsess on conversations that may have faded from public consciousness but are in no way resolved. The works of Murray Rothbard, Jack Weatherford, William Poundstone, Nassim Taleb, and John Kenneth Galbraith come immediately to mind.

Lastly, I submit a humble acknowledgement to practitioners who have played a role in my career, such as Mohamad El-Erian, Kenneth Roghoff, Carmen Reinhart, Yuval Noah Harari, Nouriel Roubini, Claude Shannon, and Edward O. Thorp. And a special note of appreciation to Dr. Arthur B. Laffer, who leads by action and demonstrates that one does not have to settle for a single interest and instead can create a livelihood out of research, publication, and asset management.

TABLE OF CONTENTS

PREFACE

The creation of music, science, literature, architecture, flower gardens, and all that tends to increase the spiritual and esthetic values of life, could hardly be possible without the accumulation of a store of wealth to support this endeavor.

—Elgin Groseclose, *Money and Man: A Survey of Monetary Experience*[1]

On Monday, November 12, 2018, the Dow Jones Industrial Average dropped 602.12 points or 2.32 percent, the S&P 500 dropped 54.79 points or 1.97 percent, and the Nasdaq dropped 206.03 points or 2.78 percent. This drop had followed an exceptionally bumpy October in the markets, with the broad indices falling into correction territory. Bitcoin—which over the year leading up to that November day in 2018 had seen sell-offs prior to market downturns—was relatively stable in October, and as of November 12, it was up 0.03 percent.

As of early 2018, I, as well as many other self-respecting market participants, would not have bothered looking at Bitcoin. It is safe to say that at that time, most people still did not know what a Bitcoin even was. Yet in that space of time, something changed. Was a revolution here to disrupt the status quo? It's often difficult to acknowledge a historical moment when we're living through it.

Indeed today, Bitcoin still seems remarkably different from the broad public market securities, as it can sometimes be difficult to determine exactly what is the "speculative" asset and what is the better "store of wealth."

Make no mistake, I am not a Bitcoin or cryptocurrency (as the myriad of digital tokens are called) fanatic set out to convert the world. Far from it. Instead, my goal is to understand the true nature of "money," where it came from, and, more importantly, where it is going.

Bitcoin is an actor in this story, just as gold, stocks, bonds, and stone discs have been before. What we are really discussing here is financial technology, or fintech as it is commonly referred to. Bitcoin and the cryptocurrency revolution are but the latest iteration of fintech. But the reason they were created, the reason any meaningful fintech is created, is the real heart of the matter.

Bitcoin is an actor in this story, just as gold, stocks, bonds, and stone discs have been before.

So why are fintech created and what purpose do they serve? This is what the following pages of this book will attempt to answer. To do this, though, we need to start at the beginning. I mean the real beginning—early humans kind of stuff.

This book is divided chronologically into four Parts. In Part I, we explore our initial relationships with money and finance and discover that who we have become has a lot to do with whom we owed. We shall examine the very profound and peculiar effects money has on our minds, for better or for worse. In Part II, we see that the discovery of pressing certain metals into tokens intermixed with the notions of individual freedom and government restraint—which all melded together in some strange alchemy to create a confused love affair with gold and silver that still plagues us to this day. Part III takes us inside the US Federal Reserve, which has dominated our monetary society for the past century. While in Part IV, we explore the new cyber frontier of money and the age-old rationale for its existence. I will argue that we have had three major fintech revolutions throughout our civilization and that we are at the very vanguard of the most recent. The question is: will this revolution have an equally dramatic or lasting legacy as the others?

> **I will argue that we have had three major fintech revolutions throughout our civilization and that we are at the very vanguard of the most recent. The question is: will this revolution have an equally dramatic or lasting legacy as the others?**

Before continuing, it is worth noting what this book is not. This book is not a text to promote or praise any of the subjects covered. Instead, I hope to guide readers through our shared financial history and offer qualitative notes on the strengths and weaknesses of the topics covered. This book is also not a conspiracy theory. Money, central banking, and cryptocurrency are topics rife with sensationalism and conspiracy theories.[2]

Instead, our journey in this text will center around the innovative financial technological breakthroughs—first money, then central banking, and ultimately Bitcoin—and the effects each has had on our society. This discussion is of importance for all of us now, as the planet evolves into an ever more complex and interconnected monetary society.

INTRODUCTION

Money: something generally accepted
as a medium of exchange, a measure
of value, or a means of payment

Revolution: a sudden, radical,
or complete change

Merriam-Webster

ithin the relatively short context of financial history, we have witnessed two great financial technologies, or fintech, that have revolutionized how humans survive, thrive, and organize society. The first was the invention of money, while the second was the advent of central banks. We are now witnessing the birth of a third great fintech that could once more revolutionize our global financial system: blockchain, first popularized by Bitcoin and other cryptocurrencies.

I intend to take readers on a journey that helps them recognize the peculiar effect money has on humans. We'll discover where money came from, understand what central banks are and how they came to rule the financial world of today, and explore the emergence of cryptocurrency and why it appears to have taken root in the popular imagination.

Why Worry about Money?

The great Harvard economist and financial historian John Kenneth Galbraith says in his book *Money: Whence It Came, Where It Went*:

> Most things in life—automobiles, mistresses, cancer—are important only to those who have them. Money, in contrast, is equally important to those who have it and those who don't. Both, accordingly, have a concern for understanding it. Both should proceed in the full confidence that they can.[3]

This statement cuts to the heart of two significant issues with money: first, there is a need to worry about it, and, second, there is a need to understand it, despite our best effort to intentionally complicate a seemingly simple subject.

Although humans have a relatively limited experience with modern financial markets (stocks, bonds, etc.) of only a few centuries, we have a rather deep experience spanning thousands of years with money itself. History is littered with well-documented cases of the power of money to build and destroy civilizations. Yet, for some reason, money continues to be viewed as too complex a thing for the lay citizens to concern themselves with. This has not always been the case. In fact, money itself has been the primary political concern of the populace throughout much of our political and social history.

Galbraith continues:

The history of money teaches much or it can be made to teach much. It is, indeed, exceedingly doubtful if much that is durable can be learned about money in any other way. Attitudes towards money proceed in long cyclical swings. When money is bad, people want it to be better. When it is good, they think of other things. Only as matters are examined over time can we see how people who are experiencing inflation yearn for stable money and how those who are accepting the discipline and the costs of stability come to accept the risks of inflation. It is this cycle that teaches us that nothing, not even inflation, is permanent. We learn also that the fear of inflation which inflation leaves in its wake can be as damaging as the inflation itself. From the history we can also see, more vividly than in any other way, how money and the techniques for its management and mismanagement were evolved and how they now serve or fail to serve.[4]

Galbraith's assessment of the value of monetary history is not a singular view. In fact, another more current Harvard professor and financial historian Niall Ferguson expressed similar statements in his book *The Ascent of Money*, as we shall see later in this book.[5] And I could not agree more with Galbraith and Ferguson. It is from this vantage point that I offer this text.

The Third Revolution: Blockchain

We are currently living through what could be another pivot point in financial technology as the world considers the role of blockchain technology and the rise of the cryptocurrencies that have begun to flourish.

Since the creation of Bitcoin, there has been a literal explosion of other cryptocurrencies based on blockchain, the technology at the heart of cryptocurrency. So, what is blockchain? According to George Gilder, blockchain is "a database, similar to a cadaster of real estate titles, extended to events, covenants, patents, licenses, or other permanent records. All are hashed together mathematically from the origin of the series, each record distributed and publicized on decentralized internet nodes."[6] Blockchain is the name given the process that occurs for the creation and storage of data processed. It is the recordkeeping technology behind Bitcoin. The name is, in effect, a simplified description of what is happening. "At its most basic level, blockchain is literally just a chain of blocks, but not in the traditional sense of those words. When we say the words "block" and "chain" in this context, we are actually talking about digital information (the "block") stored in a public database (the "chain")."[7]

If you are tilting your head in wonder or confusion, you aren't alone. We are currently witnessing society, governments, lawmakers, and regulators struggle to understand how these emergent financial technologies enter into our current social and monetary system—and even if they should.

I hope that as you read this text, you'll find the evolution of money and the role it has played through history as interesting and helpful as it was to research. Enjoy!

SECTION 1

**Monetary Society:
The Role of Money in the Formation
of Civilization and Modern Thinking**

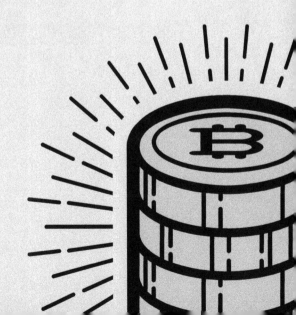

CHAPTER 1

MONETARY SOCIETY

In many ways, the twentieth century was the epoch of monetary society. The world witnessed almost unanimous adoption of money as the principal organizing structure of society. Over the preceding three centuries we moved into an era where monetary theorists could proclaim free markets, capitalism, and aligned incentives as the most effective way to improve the global population's standard of living. It was an era of unbridled privatization where the introduction of capital became the yardstick by which all facets of life should be measured. A world in which central banks and fiat currency (money without intrinsic value, backed only by the authority of a government) transitioned from innovative financial technology to the norm. Where institutions whose wisdom, authority, and control were beyond the comprehension of the average citizen and seemingly beyond rebuke.

This is in sharp contrast to prior social organizing schemas. Gone are the days of more primal organization structures such as the tribute society of Homer's *Iliad* and *Odyssey*. Religious society has served to fracture the world into legacy conflicts that continue to divide rather than unite. The ideals of communist society have long been on the wane, and communism, socialism, and the nation-state, government-centric models of society have given way to money as the central pillar of power and measure.

However, as we have transitioned into the 21st century, we are beginning to see the shortcomings of monetary societies. We can now see the structural perils of monetizing education, healthcare, and defense. We understand money's tendency to concentrate in the hands of a small cross-section of society and the politically destabilizing effects wealth inequality can bring to a civilization. Despite these cracks in the foundation of our modern society, we have traveled far enough into this paradigm that many simply cannot imagine any other forms of society.

We understand money's tendency to concentrate in the hands of a small cross-section of society and the politically destabilizing effects wealth inequality can bring to a civilization.

We are not resigned to our fates of "come what may." Instead, we have reached a level of academic awareness that allows meaningful analysis of the challenges posed by monetary society as well as comparisons of new forms of social organization that have yet to find meaningful adoption.

Obviously, evaluation of social organization itself is best left to thinkers more qualified and intelligent than I am, as well as exhaustive future debates. Before we can adequately examine social organization paradigms, however, we must first fully understand the mechanics of our current monetary society. For the purposes of this book, we will focus on understanding where we are and how we got here.

As the name implies, monetary society is one in which the organizing principle is money itself. Although many citizens throughout the world would like to quickly *rebuff* the notion that *their* framework of society is rooted in money, the hard reality is that money has become the medium of exchange that we use in all of our day-to-day interactions. Indeed, there may be a myriad of influences on how we navigate our daily lives, but increasingly the mode of such negotiation is a form of money. We measure all aspects of our lives in monetary terms. For every great debate, whether it be healthcare, education, geopolitics, immigration, space exploration, defense, or happiness, we inevitably involve money in the conversation. In fact, I challenge you to attempt to wrestle with any issue within your life without some level of involvement of money. It's hard, isn't it?

So where did money come from and how did it come to live at the center of our daily lives? More importantly, how did it come to place such an intense and outsized influence on our thinking? How did the innovation of money come to lead to the creation of a central banking network that now controls the entire global financial system? Lastly, how can awareness of this evolution lead to better financial decision-making for us all?

I imagine that there may be no better place to begin than at the beginning. By this, I do not mean the beginning of time, but a place more interesting and relevant to the discussion at hand—the beginning of the way in which we think.

CHAPTER 2

A PRIMER ON HUMAN DEVELOPMENT

Ow did we get into the complex financial world we find ourselves in now? I suggest that humans have a much longer relationship with fintech, or financial technology, than we are aware. As society organized into larger communities, the complexity of our relationships also increased significantly. How was it that the human mind was prepared for the great leap forward in mental development required for the evolution from family to tribe to community to society? Let us begin with the most basic of building blocks.

How important is the food you eat? Would you believe me if I told you that food played a meaningful role in helping enable the growth of the human brain and our emergence as the intellectual creatures we are today? As interesting as the brain is, it requires an exceptional amount of energy to power it. Neuroscientist Suzana Herculano-Houzel postulates that humans were propelled forward through an innovative technology that many of us take for granted today. The puzzle begins with the question: how did humans obtain a higher proportion of neurons relative to other animals? And further, how did humans develop a brain that consumes 25 percent more energy than other animals? If accurately compared to other animals or other primates (our closest relative comparison), humans should have far fewer neurons and spend approximately nine hours per day eating in order to fuel our brains.[8]

Suzana Herculano-Houzel suggests that humanity separated from the other animals on the planet with the invention of cooking. Indeed, the act of preparing food for consumption actually begins the process of breaking the food down or pre-digesting the food prior to consumption. This nifty innovation allowed humans to obtain higher levels of nutrients with a substantial reduction in the time required to consume and digest the food. The enhanced capacity for nutrient intake stimulated additional brain development according to Herculano-Houzel and human development began to diverge from other species.[9]

Developing more neurons and additional brain capacity in and of itself was not enough to expand our intellect to the level that we can effectively evaluate the concepts and ideas within this book. It took one additional leap forward to enable you to consider the words I put before you. We needed language.

In his book *A Thousand Days of Wonder*, psychologist Charles Fernyhough described an experiment involving rats that led to an astounding discovery of how important language is to the way we think. In the study, rats were spun around a few times to disorient them and then placed in a completely white room. Their task was simple: find a small biscuit that served as a tasty treat. Given that all four walls were completely white, the rats had no clues to help orient them and thus they enjoyed a 50 percent success rate.[10]

In an effort to improve performance, the researchers adjusted conditions by turning one of the four walls blue. Theoretically, the rats should be able to reference everything in the room to the blue wall, finding the biscuit more successfully than when the room was all white. Unfortunately for the rats, their success did not improve, and they continued to find the food only 50 percent of the time. This is not because rats can't see color; they could in fact see the blue wall. But for some reason the presence of the blue wall provided no help in locating the biscuit. *Why?*

The rats could only process the information presented to them separately, i.e. "left" or "blue," but not "left of blue." They have the mental wiring to understand directions (left or right) as well as color, but they could not link the two pieces of information together to improve their performance.

The experiment itself does not sound all that difficult to understand and the results are only mildly surprising. However, it was when humans tried the same experiment that things got interesting. When presented the same conditions, some humans could not accomplish the task.

Harvard psychologist Elizabeth Spelke has spent a great deal of time studying babies, and, at one point, she decided to replicate the same rat experiment with children. The result? Children aged five and under did no better than the original subjects. Just like the rats, the children could not connect "left or right" with "blue" to improve performance.[11]

As a parent, I also found this notion astounding—were children no smarter than rats? What was surprising and perhaps alarming was that children could not associate the two ideas until age six.

What could be behind the difference in performance when a child reaches age six? The theory, according to Spelk and Fernyhough, is that language is what enables the leap forward in thought. Granted, children learn to speak much earlier than age six, but it is at this age that they begin to use spatial language, according to Spelke. Only at the time that a child can link "left" and "blue" to form the notion "left of blue" does their performance improve and they begin to leave the rats far behind.

To quote Spelke, "Everybody has always talked about how language is this incredible tool for communication that allows us to exchange information with other people so much more richly and effectively than animals can. But language also seems to me to serve as a mechanism of communication between different systems within a single mind."[12] It seems that language literally connects isolated thoughts and ideas within a human's mind to enable enhanced thought, orientation, and adaptability.

So, what are the implications for this study? To quote Fernyhough:

> If you reflect on your own experience, if you think about what's going on inside your head as you're just walking to work or sitting on a subway train, much of what's going on in your head at that point is actually verbal. I want to suggest that the central thread of all this is actually language; it's a stream of inner speech. That's what most of us think of as thinking.[13]

Consider for a moment that the great innovative achievement that allowed humankind to shift from a reactionary creature to a predictive creature, capable of orientating the self in the world and planning ahead, is *language*. Whereas the innovation of cooking food contributed to our expanded brain capacity, the creation of language gave us *thought*, as we know it. To build upon this, capturing the exponential power of language in *written form* enabled humanity to organize society and usher in a new level of civilization.

What then, drove humanity to capture language in the written word? Was it the need to record our story or a desire to record achievements or the rules of society? Or was it something altogether different?

The Shared Origins of the Written Word, History, and Money

Archeologist David Greaber argues in his book *Debt: The First 5,000 Years* that written language was driven by the need to record contracts and trade or, better yet, *debt* among the rapidly evolving and increasingly complex economic relationships society was forming.[14] Debt, or the obligation of one person to "pay" another person, appears to have been the initial cause of the written word. When considering how much value humankind has received from the written word throughout the ages, the notion of debt being the source of this technology seems disturbingly unromantic.

This book will discuss in depth how the financial requirements of humans have continually created technological innovations that have changed the course of history. Fintech has repeatedly influenced civilization and plays a larger role in forming the world around us than many of us are aware. As historian Niall Ferguson famously said, "Financial history is the backbone of all history."[15]

Ferguson is not alone in this realization that finance underlies the larger human story. Greaber takes the argument a step further saying that complex credit systems are older than money itself and that in many ways, *debt* is the backbone of all history:

The most shocking blow to the conventional version of economic history came with the translation, first of Egyptian hieroglyphics, and then of Mesopotamian cuneiform, which pushed back scholars' knowledge of written history almost three millennia, from the time of Homer (circa 800 BC), where it had hovered in [Adam] Smith's time, to roughly 3500 BC. What these texts revealed was that credit systems . . . actually preceded the invention of coinage by thousands of years.

The Mesopotamian system is the best documented, more so than that of Pharaonic Egypt (which appears similar), Shang China (about which we know little), or the Indus Valley civilization (about which we know nothing at all). As it happens, we know a great deal about Mesopotamia, since the vast majority of cuneiform documents were financial in nature.[16]

You might find it amusing to know that Dr. Graeber's notion of written language developing from an economic need to record debts is supported by a fascinating 2011 documentary entitled *How Beer Saved the World* by Alan Eyres.[17] Eyres' film suggests that the oldest known form of written language, cuneiform, was in fact a record of beer transactions. If true, it supports Dr. Graeber's notion of economics (in this case, the beer trade) spurring the creation of the written word, and, let's face it, the idea is amusing!

What does all of this tell us? It informs our understanding of where our capacity to think, as we know it, comes from. It is our understanding of language and the inner voice we all have in our heads that enable our progression through society and, indeed, life. It is the application of this language in the written form that has enabled the growth of civilization and social organization that we all enjoy in the modern era. Lastly, it indicates that society has had a monetary theme since at least the creation of written language, as most original written language recorded financial transactions and debts that one owed to another.

Whereas we once thought language and written communication were created as an enlightened endeavor, they appear more accurately rooted in economics and debt. It is no small wonder then that economics and what we have come to know as money are the underpinnings of human history and can play such a meaningful role in our lives and thought processes. We have only recently come to know exactly how large a role economics plays in distorting our mental processes, a subject we will briefly discuss next, with a short introduction to behavioral economics.

CHAPTER 3

A BRIEF INTRODUCTION TO BEHAVIORAL ECONOMICS

As we embark on a journey into the origins of money, markets, and central banks, it is important to understand why money means so much to each of us. Although financial markets began centuries ago, our understanding of economics as it relates to the human brain is an alarmingly new science. Economic and monetary theory have been postulated upon since the time of Adam Smith and his March 9, 1776, publication of *An Inquiry into the Nature and Causes of the Wealth of Nations*,[18] but the advent of behavioral economics and applied psychology to investor motivation seems to have only gained significant traction in the mainstream economic conversation since the financial crisis of 2007–2008. Behavioral economics came into its own academically speaking in the 1980s when Nobel Laureates Daniel Kahneman and Amos Tversky raised the idea that imperfections in the market could be caused by "fallible human behavior."[19]

In 2014, Assistant Professor of Economics Nijmegen Floris Heukelom at Radboud University published *Behavioral Economics: A*

History. The book is largely a published version of his PhD dissertation and serves to chronologically guide the reader through the evolution from traditional economic epistemological foundations of economic pioneers such as Adam Smith, David Ricardo, Thomas Malthus, and James Mill to decision theory in psychology and ultimately to what is now known as behavioral economics. As Heukelom so painstakingly describes, economics itself has shifted over time, moving away from Adam's methodology for understanding the wealth of nations to become a mathematical and model-based scientific discipline for understanding "the production, consumption, and transfer of wealth" (as stated under the current definition of *economics* on Dictionary. com). As the study of economics progressed, some began to notice that economic models and mathematic equations did not always fully capture the range of actual human decisions and outcomes.[20]

As an active market participant, I personally began to notice early in my career that individuals of varying levels of wealth, experience, and education engaged in similar patterns of behavior, often counterproductive to their stated goals, and would typically chant a similar mantra: "I know I shouldn't do this, but…" Observing this phenomenon on such a wide scale during multiple market cycles, and influenced by my undergraduate background in psychology, I wanted a better understanding of the behavioral components of investment management. I began to devour the published works of Kahneman and Tversky, as well as later contributors such as Robert Shiller, George Akerlof, and Dan Ariely.

In 2009, Robert Shiller and George Akerlof (husband to former Federal Reserve Chairwoman Janet Yellen) published their breakthrough book *Animal Spirits: How Human Psychology Drives the Economy, and Why It Matters for Global Capitalism*.[21] Named after the phenomenon that famed economist John Maynard Keynes used in his 1936 book *The General Theory of Employment, Interest, and Money* to describe human emotions and economic activity, the book was both timely in its publication date and subject matter.[22] Arriving during the financial crisis of 2007–2008, a more humanistic approach to understanding bubbles and their economic effects was welcome reading for stranded investors seeking answers. I was immediately reminded of the famous quote from Walt Kelly's comic strip *Pogo*, "We have met the enemy and he is us."[23] Kelly adapted the quote from Commodore Oliver Hazard Perry after his 1813 victory on Lake Erie in the War of 1812, but the value is just the same.[24] Seeking answers for how the economy had come to such a wretched state, we are forced to look within ourselves for our "share" of responsibility.

Indeed, within the realm of money, investing, and personal finance, humans are faced with internal challenges just as complex as the outside macroeconomic environment. I suggest findings from both psychology and behavioral economics help us understand why such money revolutions as central banks and blockchain occur.

CHAPTER 4

THE MODERN RELATIONSHIP WITH MONEY

In modern society, we are continually told to invest our money. The "where" and "how" of this investing mantra vary but the theme is the same; we are told over and over again that we should invest. Of course, there is significant wisdom in prudent investing, but the mantra does not make distinctions. The importance of this concept is that even when confronted with information that makes a person uncomfortable with investing or staying invested, we are continually reinforced by authority figures to do so. I suggest that the idea of investing is sound, but that *understanding how, why, and where to invest is imperative.* Simply obeying the financial authority figures of the time is not sufficient.

To be sure, expert advice is a wonderful thing to have, but it is just that—advice. One hopes that such advice is based on rigorous analysis, sound fundamental principles, disciplined processes of research, and years of experience. However, each of us holds the responsibility to work through the issues ourselves. We can lean on experts and research to guide our thought process, but we cannot relinquish the responsibility of critical thinking to others. It is important to stress this concept because the human mind is designed to be efficient. In other words, we take mental shortcuts as often as possible.

Nobel Laureate Daniel Kahneman presents an exceptional summary of his work with Amos Tversky in his book *Thinking Fast and Slow*, which provides insight into how the human brain organizes and processes information.[25] *Thinking Fast and Slow* should be added to every reading list, as it provides exceptional evidence of how our minds work. Presenting the difference between the two systems of operations within each of us, Dr. Kahneman familiarizes us with the slow and methodical brain as well as the fast and assumptive brain within us. Our capacity to thrive and survive on this planet would largely be impossible without both systems. Whereas the slow and analytical mind is critical to our capacity to solve complex problems and move the human experience forward, it requires tremendous energy and a safe and stable environment to operate. While our fast and assumptive brain makes lightning-quick inferences and can be thanked for keeping us alive and out of danger throughout our evolution, it is prone to mistakes, some of which can be extremely damaging.

It is important to understand the differences between the mental operations that take place within our minds every second and in times of significant importance (i.e., when money is involved) and to stop and identify which system is currently driving our thoughts. As stated before, the human mind is one of the most efficient machines ever known. However, this advantage can become a weakness when we rely on it too much. More often than not, human society requires the heavy lifting of our slow and analytical mind to work through the challenges we face, whereas our internal preference for minimal effort pushes us to rely on the fast and assumptive mind, which can lead to trouble. Understanding what motivates people is the key to becoming a better investor as it allows for a better understanding of one's own tendencies and, more importantly, allows one to stay in front of the curve, thus on the profitable side of a trade.

Money on Our Mind

To compound the difficulties faced by the human mind with respect to money and investing, let's examine the differences in which we perceive success and failure and the mental consequences of each.

Consider for a moment that your internal interpretation of an outcome can have a strong influence on your subsequent decisions. How would you know that a subsequent decision was correct? Would you know if you were still utilizing the slow and methodical system of your brain and not the fast and assumptive, prone-to-error system? Make no mistake, even highly educated and experienced investment professionals are prone to the same behavioral weaknesses that plague the average investor. The difference is that professionals follow disciplined processes for decision-making in an attempt to mitigate behavioral economic tendencies.

One such tendency has received a good amount of study—the significance of *loss aversion*. Initially proposed by Daniel Kahneman and Amos Tversky in their 1979 work "Prospect Theory: An Analysis of Decision under Risk," the pair noted that "losses loom larger than gains" within the human mind.[26] The net effect of their studies on gain/loss perception resulted in the observation that a loss emotionally affects humans two and a half times more than an equal gain. In other words, losing $1,000 has a negative emotional effect that is only counterbalanced by a positive emotional effect associated with a gain of $2,500. Clearly, we feel good with gains but feel much more intensity with respect to losses. Moreover, to alleviate the negative emotional effects of a loss, we must experience a gain of 2.5 times our loss (a feat not always easy to come by). The lesson to be gleaned from this by both investor and advisor is that humans are intrinsically motivated to avoid losses by a greater drive than they are to obtain gains.

So, what does this mean with respect to portfolio management? It suggests that greater effort should be devoted to minimizing the risk of loss than to maximizing gains. In modern terms, more conservative investment objectives and/or greater use of hedging strategies will most likely protect the investor's emotional state and, thus, their potential for maintaining rationality.

Before we leave the topic of behavioral economics, it is important to recognize the basis for the most common investor instincts. All investors recognize risk when they set out on their investment journey. They understand that it exists and are willing to take on some degree of it in exchange for their perceived potential gain. However, when they are directly exposed to losses, a basic human instinct kicks in. Imagine the age-old survival phenomenon known as "fight or flight." In this psychological paradigm, a creature reverts to one of two options when faced with danger: it either fights the perceived aggressor or runs as fast as it can. What many people have yet to recognize is that the modern social and financial system has integrated money and investments into the human being's basic hierarchy of needs. For better or worse, we now live in a monetary society and, within such a context, some heretofore classic paradigms may now be viewed in a new light.

Abraham Maslow introduced the hierarchy of needs theory in his 1943 paper "A Theory of Human Motivation."[27] This pyramid chart illustrates Maslow's understanding of what is most important to human survival and thus what motivates humans as they move through life.

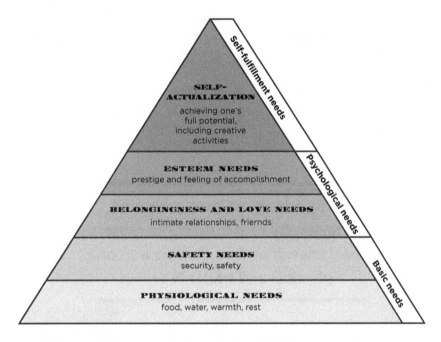

At the base of the pyramid are those needs that are of maximum importance to a human's basic survival. The two most important are physiological needs, such as food and water, and safety needs, such as security and shelter.

It is my argument that in monetary society, there exists one physical representation of both of these most vital human needs (which are also humanity's strongest motivators). The advent of money allowed humanity to symbolize its most basic needs and motivators into one physical and tradable object. Since that time, humanity has developed several ways in which to gather, store, and increase the physical supply of its "needs symbol."

As time progressed, society as a whole has shifted to embrace this single symbol as the fundamental basis for the exchange of all goods and services, thus elevating the status of the "needs symbol" to its present-day, end-all, be-all representation of a human's capacity to survive and thrive in this world. Moreover, the past century has ushered in an era in which monetary society is the dominant society globally. Although there remain some small communities and cultures that cling to alternative social structures, monetary societies have become the rule du jour—for better or worse. Indeed, money really does make the world go round.

The advent of money allowed humanity to symbolize its most basic needs and motivators into one physical and tradable object.

Thus, investing, in general, has taken on significant importance to humans as they view the gains and losses of investing as detrimental to their own capacity to survive and/or thrive. When the markets are moving up and overall monetary wealth is increasing, humans become quite euphoric as they translate that movement into more food, more shelter, and more safety. Ultimately, they feel fat and happy. However, when markets move down, investors suddenly feel their capacity to survive is threatened and they begin to panic, reverting to the age-old options of "fight or flight." However, most investors do not understand how to "fight" financially. Thereby, the overwhelming majority seeks the second option of "flight." In financial markets, "flight" is constituted by panic selling—getting out at all costs—in order to shift their assets to "safe" investment vehicles where the investor can at least achieve some level of predictability with respect to the storage of money, and thus the capacity to survive.

This is why we see such tremendous volatility in unstable markets or markets faced with less than pleasant prospects. Investors are greedy to obtain plenty, but when faced with loss, they truly begin, on a subconscious level at least, to feel their survival is threatened. This relationship between humans and money or investments is why, despite reason, investors feel compelled to execute bad investment decisions when they self-admittedly "know better."

To further enhance our understanding of the relationship between money and survival in the human mind, it is worth considering the research described in Dan Ariely and Jeff Kreisler's latest book, *Dollars and Sense: How We Misthink Money and How to Spend Smarter.*[28] Within this book, the authors point out several of the mental conditions that work against our desire for thrift in an environment that is increasingly stacked against us, tempting us to spend and consume. To highlight the relationship our minds have with money, *Washington Post* contributor Michelle Singletary references Ariely's and Kreisler's work, noting: "studies using neuroimaging and MRIs [that] show that paying stimulates the same brain regions that process physical pain."[29]

We know money woes can stimulate a pain response. But can money also relieve pain? This phenomenon was illustrated in a research paper published in the June 2009 edition of the journal *Psychological Science*. Research participants were split into two groups, one who would count paper money of large denominations and the other who would count only blank pieces of paper. Both groups were then subjected to a research assistant strapping down their arm and dipping their fingers into a bowl of hot water at a temperature of 122 degrees Fahrenheit or 50 degrees Celsius. The result was that *those who had counted money prior to the experiment rated their pain lower than those who counted paper.*[30]

Kathleen Vohs, of the University of Minnesota and coauthor of the study noted, "These effects speak to the power of money, even as a symbol, to change perceptions of very real feelings," like pain. Such a discovery stands to bolster the overwhelming impact money has on human psychology and motivation and helps illustrate the importance of understanding these connections and how they affect market participation.[31]

In other words, money has the power to both cause and relieve human pain, or at least our mind processes it in such a way that the results are indistinguishable. The notion that money has come to drive such intense responses from our brains is perhaps one of the most important lessons of this text. We are not the rational, levelheaded creatures we fancy ourselves to be. In fact, we are operating off of mental impulses that are beyond our consciousness and have unprecedented influence on our decision-making and our capacity to thrive and survive in our monetary society.

As a result of continued study of the human mind and emotions when dealing with money, I have provided evidence that suggests that the entire lower blocks of Maslow's hierarchy of needs can effectively be symbolized in today's society as money. The importance of money to the human psyche as the physical representation of physiological needs, safety needs, belonging and love needs, and esteem needs can't be underestimated. The psychological connections with money inside the human brain illustrate why investors behave badly, bubbles occur, and markets will remain irrational. These even contribute to fintech disruptions—for instance, Bitcoin's ascendence in the post-2008 Great Recession.

In short, it can be summarized that money can, in fact, "short circuit" our brains and cause the individual to act in surprising ways.

The great Dan Ariely, a behavioral economist at Duke University, has written extensively on the subject of humans behaving badly and has shared numerous studies that illustrate some of our internal flaws when dealing with money. One such study shared in his 2008 book *Predictably Irrational: The Hidden Forces That Shape Our Decisions* immediately seems relevant and is one that relates to optionality and our drive to keep our options open even to our own detriment.[32]

Dr. Ariely devised a methodology to tease out the effects of optionality on our decision-making process. Ariely designed a computer game in which participants navigated through doors into rooms to obtain points. Although he designed several variations to establish control groups and isolate behaviors, the crux of the study illustrated that individuals would operate in a fashion contrary to their economic benefit (i.e., the pursuit of highest point values) just to keep their available choices open. The game had three doors that players could click on to obtain points. If a player did not click on a door after a period of time, that door would lock and would no longer be available as an option for the player to choose. Each click on a door presented the player with a certain number of points. Even when the game was rigged to pay out much higher point values to players that continued clicking on one specific door, the players could not help themselves from clicking on a "lower value" door when they feared that it might become locked and thus eliminated from their available options.[33]

Dr. Ariely's study was quite remarkable in demonstrating exactly how important maintaining choices is to an individual. Within the confines of an isolated study presented to participants as a game, individuals willingly penalized themselves financially to keep their options open and simultaneously avoided commitment to a single course of action despite clear awareness of the economic values such a commitment would bring them.

It begs the question: *why?* Why would reasonable individuals choose to set aside immediate economic benefit to ensure that they retained multiple options? Fortunately, the study offers room for speculation on what compulsions were at work within the mind, not the least of which was risk aversion. Regardless of the information pattern presented by the game, players intuitively took steps to keep alternative doors open in the event the paradigm shifted or, in other words, risk occurred. But this was not the only motivation at work. As the game evolved, it became clear that participants could not stand the immediate pain of loss associated with an option being taken away.

The significance of Dr. Ariely's study was to illustrate how important loss aversion and choice maximization are to individuals despite isolating the consequences to a simple computer game. For better or worse, these behavioral instincts are hardwired into the human mind, and overpowering such tendencies can be a challenge, especially when real money is at stake.

New York Times columnist John Tierney wrote a summary of the experiment conducted by Dan Ariely and his collaborator Jiwoong Shin in 2008. Tierney correctly observed the underlying motive of players, albeit at an unconscious level:

They plumbed the players' motivations by introducing yet another twist. This time, even if a door vanished from the screen, players could make it reappear whenever they wanted. But even when they knew it would not cost anything to make the door reappear, they still kept frantically trying to prevent doors from vanishing.

Apparently, they did not care so much about maintaining flexibility in the future. What really motivated them was the desire to avoid the immediate pain of watching a door close.

"Closing a door on an option is experienced as a loss, and people are willing to pay a price to avoid the emotion of loss," Dr. Ariely says. In the experiment, the price was easy to measure in lost cash. In life, the costs are less obvious—wasted time, missed opportunities.[34]

Given that we are clever creatures, we tell ourselves that we make selections to keep our options open to maintain maximum future flexibility. However, it appears the real motivation within us is to avoid the pain of loss.

So then, is the effect of money on the human mind all bad? Surely the innovation of money has served some good, correct? I would be the first to emphatically agree! Naturally, the almost primal, instinctual drive that money evokes in our species has also been a tremendous motivator, creating, as byproducts of economic activity, the incredible world we see around us. In 1928, Earnest Calkins wrote an early business book titled *Business: The Civilizer*; however, I would contend that it is, in fact, money that is the great civilizer, for few mechanisms have done more to interconnect, unite, improve, or impoverish societies and individuals than money. [35]

The Transitory Nature of Money

Throughout this text, I will attempt to illustrate that money was the first and greatest financial technology, followed closely by central banking as the second. In many ways, it was these two creations that enabled the world we live in today. However, throughout the past millennia, many varying things have been used as money, which has allowed some degree of confusion among modern market participants as to exactly what defines money today.

Throughout the past millennia, many varying things have been used as money, which has allowed some degree of confusion among modern market participants as to exactly what defines money today.

I suspect that many readers will quickly come up with two phrases when thinking about the question "what is money?" The first tends to be "a medium of exchange" and the second is "a store of value." It is agreed that among the many characteristics of money, one is certainly a medium of exchange. Money has become the primary facility through which most goods and services are exchanged throughout the world. The problem lies within the second common description of money: money is "a store of value."

On a short-term basis, money will retain value, but over any measurable period of time, it has a curious susceptibility to the erosion of value. There are multiple forces that contribute to the erosion of money's value, not least of which is inflation. What makes money itself applicable in our day-to-day lives is the common belief amongst users within a society that others will accept their money in exchange for goods and services. Two primary forces foster this belief: the first is that the government of said society declares an item to be "money" and the second is society's experience of that item's success being accepted by others as "money." This paradigm that fulfills society's beliefs is a delicate balance, to say the least, and is not always reliable.

There are multiple instances within our monetary history of governments altering, suspending, and even terminating items that had previously circulated as money and rendering such items "worthless." Countries have repeatedly made both subtle and abrupt adjustments from silver coinage as money to gold coinage, and even to copper coinage when it suited the treasury's needs. Great Britain in the late seventeenth and early eighteenth centuries is one such example, while a more recent example would be the United States' abandonment of the gold standard in 1933 or the Nixon Shock of 1971 in which President Richard Nixon declared that the United States dollar was no longer redeemable for gold. Other countries have experienced bouts of hyperinflation and have made extreme currency switches in an effort to manage a destructive loss of confidence in the country's monetary system, such as Argentina in 2001 when the government froze all bank accounts and then made a mandatory conversion to a new form of the peso at a valuation 75 percent lower.[36]

I raise this point early within this book to attempt to illustrate the transitory nature of money. Within investment markets, some trends or changes can occur at a pace sufficiently slow enough or subtle enough to escape the attention of the human mind, which operates understandably on shorter time frames. Humans have largely succeeded in survival on this planet due to our capacity to identify patterns and adjust behaviors to thrive despite the volatile and often dangerous world around us.

However, with respect to money, we have a peculiar tendency to repeat past mistakes over and over again. Daniel Kahneman and Amos Tversky have done a tremendous amount of pioneering research into the mechanics of how humans deal with the world and our decision-making within it. There is simply too much information in the world around us for our brains to process all of it. So, instead, our brains create shortcuts to help make meaningful decisions in a veritable ocean of information and sensory inputs. However, a dangerous byproduct of our shortcut thinking is the creation of cognitive biases.

Money and Cognitive Biases

Before leaving the subject of behavioral economics, I would be remiss if I did not arm readers with a brief description of the types of cognitive biases that affect us the most. Biases exist primarily because of the failure of the mind to keep what is happening to us in the correct perspective. When dealing with financial assets, it is too easy for us to drift away from financial thinking into emotional or confused logic.

We have seen how money plays tricks on the human mind as well as the outsized role loss aversion plays on our subconscious. Let us now quickly review the other most common pitfalls of the human mind when it comes to investing.

First things first, cognitive biases are preconceived notions that exist within all of us and can seriously affect our judgments and decisions. This is important because each fintech revolution seems to complicate the landscape for the individual.

The same biases that have helped us survive on this planet tend to hurt us with respect to financial decision-making, sometimes leading to spectacular financial folly commonly referred to as "bubbles."

In the investment management community, the core biases as indicated by the 2017 College for Financial Planning text *Modern Portfolio Theory and Performance Evaluation of Equities* are:

- Loss aversion
- Fear of regret
- Overconfidence (optimism bias)
- Representativeness
- Framing
- Rationalization or confirmation bias
- Hindsight bias
- Self-attribution bias
- Anchoring
- Mental accounting
- Money illusion
- Availability bias
- Status quo bias
- Illusion of control bias
- Endowment bias
- Recency bias

Let's look at five of these to understand how biases inform our relationship with money.

FRAMING

Framing is the bias that describes how the way in which something is presented to us can influence the way we judge it. A quick example is to consider an item going on sale. It is more tempting to our minds to view something as having a discount, rather than a store stating that during a period of time the price will be higher than normal. The way in which we view a financial decision can be meaningfully changed based on how the information is delivered to us, independent of the information itself. This is an important item for daily consideration as we make decisions to deploy money.

ANCHORING

Anchoring refers to our tendency to fixate on a particular idea and not adequately adjust to new information. This can take the form of over-relying on social norms, relying on current trends because they are broadly accepted, or inappropriately fixating on an initial piece of information. A primary example in our day-to-day lives revolves around prices. When one becomes inclined to make a purchase, the first price they view the item at becomes an anchor. All future references will be viewed in terms of this initial price. In the case of purchasing cereal, the implications of anchoring can be small whereas in the case of purchasing a home, anchoring to the initial price can be a costly mistake. For all things one can buy, determining value is a tricky process. Awareness of our vulnerability towards anchoring can help reset one's perspective and lead to substantially improved decision-making.

MONEY ILLUSION

Perhaps the most devastating bias in our modern economy is money illusion. This is the bias for humans to misunderstand the effects of inflation. We have a tendency to ignore the effects of inflation or at best to underestimate the role inflation plays in our financial decisions. When faced with a choice between a low-interest rate and a low inflation rate versus a high-interest rate and a high inflation rate, we tend to prefer the higher numbers regardless of what the actual "real" return is. This means we focus more on the nominal information than the "real" result. For example, a 2 percent interest rate in a zero percent inflationary environment will be unfairly deemed less attractive than a 6 percent rate in a 4 percent inflationary environment. Clearly, the results are identical, but our minds fail to accurately balance all of the important information. A more important effect is the tendency for us to view an investment in a federally insured certificate of deposit (CD) as "safer" than an investment that may carry price fluctuations but higher overall returns. We discount the effect of inflation on purchasing power for the "safe" investment because we cannot easily see the effects. The erosion of purchasing power is not printed on our financial statements as is the "mark-to-market" pricing changes on "riskier" security. This can lead an investor to falsely assume they are making prudent decisions to invest "safely" while blindly losing the bulk of their wealth to the erosive effects of long-term inflation.

STATUS QUO BIAS

I grew up in Appalachia and a common phrase in our vernacular is "if it ain't broke, don't fix it." In physics, this can be referred to as inertia, the tendency of the current scenario to continue. When faced with incoming information that suggests a high degree of uncertainty, it is far easier to do nothing than to make a change and risk being wrong. Similarly, according to Newton's first law, objects at rest tend to stay at rest, and objects in motion tend to stay in motion unless acted upon by an outside force. In the realm of finance, our tendency towards the *status quo bias generally means that we participate in extreme moves, despite our better judgment, because that is where the momentum of the herd is going. It is mentally easier to ride the market than to exert force, execute a change, and exit the herd.*

RECENCY BIAS

In my view, recency bias is perhaps the most dangerous bias in financial markets and is in large part an underlying theme of this book. Recency bias is our tendency to place higher importance on our most recent experiences than the broader historical wealth of information. We tend to speculate future events based primarily on what we have most recently witnessed or experienced. Mark Twain is thought to have said, "history doesn't repeat itself, but it often rhymes." This idea is rooted in this specific bias. We have a tendency not to pay attention to historical lessons and instead get mentally bogged down in current events and recent experiences. This tendency subjects us to irrational behavioral decisions that increase the likelihood we will make similar mistakes as we have in the past.

Evolutionarily speaking, survival on this planet required us to adapt to our immediate environment, not the environment of the past. The efficiency of our minds accounted for this survival need by placing higher emphasis with regards to memory and physical response to the most recent experience rather than historical experiences. In simplified terms, recency gives us instinct while history gives us wisdom.

As we have discussed, recency bias is the tendency for humans to assume that what has happened to us most recently is likely to be what happens again in the future. Although this bias can obviously contribute to the financial market's tendency to overshoot—in other words, go up higher than is rational in good times and go down lower than is rational in bad times—it also distorts our understanding of money itself. Indeed, we tend to think of money as a more permanent object of utility in our day-to-day lives because it has been so in our prior experiences (often lifetimes). That is to say that because money so effectively purchased all of our required goods and services throughout our recent memory, we assume it will continue to do so.

> **Because money so effectively purchased all of our required goods and services throughout our recent memory, we assume it will continue to do so.**

However, in reality, money does not buy the same things in exchange for the same quantity year in and year out. Granted, a US citizen likely purchased a gallon of milk using similar-looking dollars five years ago as today, but they did not make the purchase for the exact same amount of dollars. Clearly, we all understand this to be the work of inflation and the concept comes as no surprise. Yet, again, when asked "what is money?" most people tend to believe it to be a store of value. I suggest that day-to-day users of money should better understand the nature of money, which, in turn, will help them better understand investing (the only true way to create a "store of value") and therefore increase their capacity to survive and thrive in the current era of our monetary society.

So how did we get to a place where money prevails through all facets of our lives? We have not always lived within a monetary society. In fact, monetary society is a relatively new phenomenon and has only recently become the dominant social order on the planet. The concept can be difficult to grasp, especially for students in Western educational systems, as the monetary society seems to have always been there. However, for the bulk of society's history, the organizing principles were anything but monetary based. The world has witnessed religious societies, agricultural societies, warring societies, slaving societies, and others, many of which held sway for periods of time far longer than that of monetary society's reign. Yet, the world has now come to be dominated by the monetary system with a plethora of academic and political disciplines to justify and promote its virtues.

I previously mentioned Adam Smith's work *An Inquiry into the Nature and Causes of the Wealth of Nations.* Smith referred to an invisible hand that helped facilitate equilibrium between supply and demand, setting in motion a legacy of the indisputable harmony and legitimacy of economics in human society. Clearly, Smith's work initiated a seismic shift in power in the world from kings, queens, and religions to commerce and industry. Given the influence of money on society, it is important to understand where the technological invention of money comes from and how the institutions that now control the supply of money came to dominate the modern world.

SECTION 2

The History of Money and Central Banking

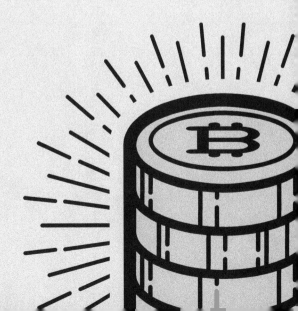

CHAPTER 5

A TIME BEFORE CENTRAL BANKS

What is a central bank and where did they come from? More importantly, how did they come to rule the world? To understand central banking, it is critical to understand money itself.

Referring to money as "currency" is a relatively new practice, dating back to the early 1700s, when money was first noted to have a "flow" about it. Specifically, some countries were observed to have very little "specie" or available physical monetary units (bills and coins) available to the populace despite a government that was active in creating and distributing physical money. How could this be? It was observed that the money seemed to "flow" away from some regions and "flow" into others. This peculiar and, at the time, unexplainable process lent to money similar characteristics as water flowing through rivers and seas—hence the adoption of the word "currency" to describe both the movement of money and the money itself.

It was only a small mental leap to perceive that there could or should be an entity that controls such a current. This idea is what gave rise to what we have come to know as a central bank.

Central banking, at its core, sets and maintains monetary policy for a given country or economic region. Investopedia defines monetary policy as "the actions of a central bank, currency board, or other regulatory committee that determine the size and rate of growth of the money supply, which in turn affects interest rates. Monetary policy is maintained through actions such as modifying the interest rate, buying or selling government bonds, and changing the amount of money banks are required to keep in the vault (bank reserves)."[37] Think of monetary policy as controlling the amount, flow, and value of money. A central banker has no less importance to the world of men than the force that controls the amount and flow of water through the streams, rivers, and seas!

So then, what is money? Obviously, most people immediately think of coins and paper money when they imagine what money is. However, with just a bit of reflection, everyone can quickly picture various forms of alternative money that have been utilized throughout history. From salt, silk, and tobacco to the cowrie shells of Africa and the wampum of the Native Americans, humans have utilized all sorts of items for money. In fact, the common slang word "buck" used for the American dollar is a direct descendant of the frontier usage of buckskins, or furs, as a form of currency.

The nature of money has been debated for centuries.

The nature of money has been debated for centuries, with a common narrative suggesting that money evolved as the logical next step from the barter system, wherein those wishing to transact trade found it necessary to introduce a medium of exchange, often in the form of metal coins that would be widely accepted as a go-between for the items they wished to sell and the items they wished to buy. This idea of how money came to be has been so widely repeated that it has become, to many, the undisputed truth.

In reality, money has had a much more interesting history, full of conflict, and is, in itself, closer to a concept than a physical item. Indeed, the great economist Milton Friedman noted the inconsistency of the "from barter to coin" version of money's history in his 1992 work *Money Mischief: Episodes in Monetary History*.[38] Friedman begins this great work with a reference to William Henry Furness III, who introduced the Western world to the island of Yap, a small island within the Caroline Islands of Micronesia. Here, a particular medium of exchange called *fei* was found, and Furness talks about it in his 1910 book *The Island of Stone Money*.

Furness noted with curiosity that the medium of exchange and store of value for the inhabitants of Yap were "large, solid, thick stone wheels, ranging in diameter from a foot to twelve feet, having in the center a hole varying in size with the diameter of the stone, wherein a pole may be inserted sufficiently large and strong to bear the weight and facilitate transportation."[39]

The stones were quarried out of limestone on an island four hundred miles away and were brought to Yap by early navigators and entrepreneurs. Furness went on to describe the especially peculiar part of the stone currency:

> Another noteworthy feature of this stone currency . . . is that it is not necessary for its owner to reduce it to possession.

After concluding a bargain, which involves the price of a *fei* too large to be conveniently moved, its new owner is quite content to accept the bare acknowledgement of ownership and without so much as a mark to indicate the exchange, the coin remains undisturbed on the former owner's premises.

My faithful old friend, Fatumak, assured me that there was in the village nearby a family whose wealth was unquestioned—acknowledged by every one—and yet no one, not even the family itself, had ever laid eye or hand on this wealth; it consisted of an enormous *fei*, whereof the size is known only by tradition, for the past two or three generations it had been, and at that very time it was lying at the bottom of the sea! ... The purchasing power of that stone remains, therefore, as valid as if it were leaning visibly against the side of the owner's house.[40]

Many of you may ask: why did the great Milton Friedman focus the beginning of his book on such a "primitive" and "silly" system as that of Yap? After all, the Western world of the 1990s, when Friedman was writing, was so much more developed and evolved in monetary theory and policy.

Friedman quickly points out that we are perhaps not too far from the islanders by reminding us of how we view our own ownership of capital. Friedman highlights the behaviors of the Bank of France from 1932 to 1933, a period of time in which the Bank of France feared the US may abandon the gold standard and suspend allegiance to the traditional price of $20.67 per ounce of gold. Accordingly, the Bank of France instructed the Federal Reserve Bank of New York to shift the bulk of their dollar reserves into gold. However, instead of dealing with the headache and costs of shipping the gold to France, the Fed was instructed to put the gold on France's account. Thus, agents of the Federal Reserve went into their vault and marked the appropriate amount of gold as now belonging to the Bank of France.[41]

Money relies more on belief and confidence than physical properties, and thus money is just as much a social science as it is an economic science.

As we consider the similarities and differences between the *fei* of Yap and the gold of France, it is clear that money is far more complex than at first glance. In fact, money relies more on belief and confidence than physical properties, and thus money is just as much a social science as it is an economic science. Friedman correctly points out that in most cases, money works simply because the user believes it will be accepted in similar proportionate value by others! Friedman indicates that the US, or any other country, could hardly operate without a common and widely accepted forms of exchange, and that this exchange . . .

> . . . rests on convention: our whole monetary system owes its existence to the mutual acceptance of what, from one point of view, is no more than fiction. That fiction is no fragile thing. On the contrary, the value of having common money is so great that people will stick to the fiction even under extreme provocation. But neither is the fiction

indestructible: the phrase "not worth a Continental" is a reminder of how the fiction was destroyed by the excessive amount of Continental currency the Continental Congress issued to finance the American Revolution.[42]

Friedman's statement may be highly shocking to those unfamiliar with monetary policy and central banking. Indeed, money has become such a tremendous force in each of our lives that we are often deeply disturbed when discussing that the value and "realness" of our wealth are both questionable and resting on a fiction of sorts.

Within any society, there exists a methodology of obtaining the goods one needs to survive and thrive. Common Western belief suggests that primitive societies bartered, traded one good for another, and then, as they evolved, necessarily introduced a monetary form of exchange. However, this idea of the evolution of money is categorically false. In fact, in 1935, Dr. Elgin Groseclose wrote an in-depth description of money throughout the ages of humankind in response to a question posed to him by Joseph A. Brandt, then editor of the University of Oklahoma Press, in regards to the extreme devaluation of the dollar that followed the 1929 stock market crash and the events that made such a devaluation necessary. Dr. Groseclose summarized an alarming gap in monetary scholarship that existed at the time by stating:

It was evident that an explanation of these happenings could not be reached through any of the monetary theories then current, all of them in eclipse with the collapse of the economic structure following the Great Crash of the stock market in 1929. A deeper examination was necessary, one that went to the nature of man's experience with money. A survey of this experience was indicated. What wisdom did the records offer?

The library shelves held an endless array of works devoted to the theories of money; only an insignificant number treated its history. Few went back beyond the times of Adam Smith for either theory or experience. Most textbooks, even today, treat the development of monetary experience as proceeding from barter to money to the institutions of credit. Yet, as the archeological evidence from Mesopotamia makes clear, institutions of credit were fully developed before those of money.[43]

Alarmingly, over half a century after he wrote those words and almost a century since his first edition of the book, there remain too few widespread texts dedicated to the topic. More alarmingly, the pesky and incorrect notion of the evolution of money remains firm in the minds of the populace (including many experts and professors at large). In modern economics classes and textbooks, the introduction of economics and the evolution of money are still explained by starting with barter. But why? Why has this financial historical fallacy continued to flourish?

David Graeber contends that it has more to do with the roots of the economics discipline and Western society's political ideals than historical truth. Graeber states:

There is a simple reason why everyone who writes an economics textbook feels they have to tell us the same story. For economists, it is in a very real sense the most important story ever told. It was by telling it, in the significant year of 1776, that Adam Smith, professor of moral philosophy at the University of Glasgow, effectively brought the discipline of economics into being.

He did not make up the story entirely out of whole cloth. Already in 330 BC, Aristotle was speculating along vaguely similar lines in his treatise on politics… Adam Smith, on the other hand, was determined to overturn the conventional wisdom of his day. Above all, he objected to the notion that money was a creation of government. In this, Smith was the intellectual heir of the Liberal tradition of philosophers like John Locke, who had argued that government begins in the need to protect private property and operated best when it tried to limit itself to that function. Smith expanded on the argument, insisting that property, money, and markets not only existed before political institutions but also were the very foundation of human society. It followed insofar as government should play a role in monetary affairs, it should limit itself to guaranteeing the soundness of the currency. It was only by making such an argument that he could insist that economics is itself a field of human inquiry with its own principles and laws—that is, as distinct from, say ethics or politics.[44]

Graeber contends that the creation and retelling of the barter story "played a crucial role not only in founding the discipline of economics but in the very idea that there was something called "the economy," which operated by its own rules separate from moral or political life, and that economists could take as their field of study."[45]

It is not lost on us that Smith's writing had such a profound effect on how those who followed him thought about money, markets, and exchange. In fact, the "invisible hand" of the market became an intangible force against which one could not argue, and thus it elevated the nature of economics from a new science to an almost religious or sovereign realm.

It is also not surprising that the new notion of economics was born in England. Daron Acemoglu and James A. Robinson point out in their work *Why Nations Fail* that the Glorious Revolution of 1688 in England ushered in a political framework allowing for inclusive economic and political systems.[46] It was precisely this small initial difference in political and economic institutions that led to an overwhelming difference in growth acceleration over the following century between England and the other countries of the world. The foundation of an inclusive political system coupled with an inclusive economic system that had appropriate property rights and incentives for innovation allowed England to develop into an economic powerhouse. It was from within this realm of advanced political and economic growth that Smith was able to claim, in John Locke fashion, his notion of economics as being independent of sovereign authority, whereas would-be theorists living in most other parts of the world at that time could hardly have been so bold.

In welcomed relief to the traditional economic story that begins with barter, a recent publication titled *Money: The Unauthorized Biography* by Felix Martin picks up where David Graeber and Milton Friedman leave off regarding the lessons learned from the island of Yap and discusses in detail the nature of money. Martin shares the birth of a philosophical debate regarding monetary policy that was famously set in motion by none other than John Locke and continues in monetary debates to this day. Martin states, "We think we know what money is. We use it every day and our lives are unimaginable without it. But look more closely and you find that coins and dollar bills aren't 'real.' They're promises, symbols, and ideas. Exactly what money is has evolved enormously over the ages."[47]

Martin sets out to map the evolution of the monetary belief system in which we continue to operate. Although his book is well worth the time of any person interested in monetary policy, our focus of immediate concern will dwell on the establishment of the central banking construct that emerged in what he named "The Great Monetary Settlement." But before we dive into the compromise that changed the world, it is important to understand the conditions of finance in Europe and the monetary conversation occurring across the globe in the years leading up to the dawn of central banking.

CHAPTER 6

THE BIRTH
OF MONETARY
PHILOSOPHY

Ancient Greece is often viewed as the birth of Western philosophy and wisdom, but it was not a fully functioning monetary society. The Greeks, however, do offer an incredible description of a fully developed society *adopting* money and transitioning *into* a monetary society with voluminous records for historians to analyze. As Dr. Elgin Groseclose describes, "The introduction of coined money in Europe appears to have occurred toward the end of the eighth century BC. The evidence leads us to believe that it did not spring full blown from the inventive genius of the Greeks, but rather that it was the adoption by the ruling powers of a desirable and somewhat obvious step in the simplification of commercial dealings."[48] With continued research in the many years since Dr. Groseclose's writing, a narrower range has been established for the creation of money.

Many scholars are attracted to crediting the Greeks with the birth of money, as there exists a reasonable amount of documentation by philosophically minded people describing the transition from a society and economy without money to a fully functioning monetary society on a massive scale. Jack Weatherford, in his book *The History of Money*, quoted Voltaire as saying, "Agamemnon might have had a treasure, but certainly no money," referring to the leader of the Greek armed forces who pursued the beauty Helen to the walls of Troy and, with the help of Achilles, brought down the city in Homer's Iliad."[49] It was very near those infamous walls of Troy that the technological innovation of money really began in the little-known kingdom of Lydia.

The Greeks offer an incredible description of a fully developed society *adopting* money and transitioning *into* a monetary society with voluminous records for historians to analyze.

Although usage of nuggets composed of various metals was used from time to time, the actual stamping of these nuggets into a uniform disc-shaped unit of value declared by the sovereign did not occur until the creativity of the kingdom of Lydia. There the first minted coins were created, starting a financial revolution that continues to grip the world today. Knowing precisely who deserves the historical credit for inventing money is difficult, but Jack Weatherford says that "although something similar to money and something resembling markets can be found in Mesopotamia, China, Egypt, and many other parts of the world, they did not actually use coins until the rise of Lydia and the subsequent minting of the first coins, between 640 and 630 BC."[50] The kingdom of Lydia is not a highly familiar name to most readers these days. In fact, very little is remembered of the existence of the Lydian kingdom except for the phrase "As rich as Croesus," an expression in Turkish and English still in use today.[51] This phrase was adopted due to the prolific wealth accumulated by King Croesus during his reign of 560–546 BC.[52]

To build upon the narrative of Croesus, Peter Bernstein notes in his book *The Power of Gold: The History of an Obsession*, "According to Herodotus, the kings of Lydia traced their ancestry from Hercules and had ruled for twenty-two generations, or five hundred and fifty years."[53] Croesus, descending from this great lineage, however, was the single Lydian king whose name continues to this day. Despite inheriting the fintech innovation of coinage as a technological advance in commerce, King Croesus took steps to standardize the size and weight of his state-sponsored money, streamlining the process of trade and stimulating an economic advantage and arguably a boom within his economy.

Croesus and the kingdom of Lydia grew immensely wealthy and powerful in an era of conquest not by the tip of a sword, but through financial innovation and trade. Following the creation of Lydia's lion head-stamped coins, another commercial revolution took place through the creation of the retail market. Jack Weatherford has traced the transition from buyers and sellers seeking each other out within a community to the creation of a central place of exchange by the kings of Sardis in the late seventh century BC, which served as the model for Western civilization from the Greek agora, to medieval markets, and finally all the way to the modern shopping malls of the US.[54] Despite these incredible financial innovations, the kingdom of Lydia was ultimately lost in history. In true modern fashion, the vast wealth of the Lydian kingdom was spent faster than it could be accumulated. Ultimately, the wealth of Lydia evaporated into the sands of time, but their financial innovations survived and began to take hold in a time and place still remembered and respected for the philosophical contributions made to the Western world.

The Coinage Revolution

Although we are aware of Lydia's role in the invention of coinage as well as Eastern and Middle Eastern uses of coinage and paper money, the remainder of this text focuses on the development of Western civilization's experience with the rise of money and the Monetary Revolution. Indeed, Persia contributed immensely to the development of bills of exchange, credit practices, and philosophy, while China pioneered paper money, or fiat money—and both did so long before their Western counterparts. To be sure, myself and others will continue to produce research and works encompassing the rise of money in a broader context, which should not be missed. However, the larger volume of historical records and the peculiar characteristics of the Greek monetary experience serve as both a valuable point of study as well as a convenient "starting point" in the Western story of money.

Felix Martin contends that as coinage entered the Greek culture and economy, an important step was taken in monetary philosophy as the concept of economic value was established. Economic value assigned a system of valuation to various goods and services and allowed for a more efficient system of comparative exchange. Instead of engaging in bartering or a more complex system of paying tributes, economic participants could translate a given item or action and assign it a value in a standardized format of coinage. The benefits of standardizing value are arguably some of the most powerful contributions coinage offered ancient economies, just as standardized measurements of distance, time, and weight were to civilization centuries later.

Although Greek society embraced the use of a currency as a means to transact, their documented thoughts of organizing monetary policy were ambiguous at best. Aristotle devoted little guidance on the politics of money and Plato's contributions to the conversation were limited to recommending two currencies, one coinage for domestic transactions and a second one for international trade "to better prevent the import of foreign luxuries to his austere communal paradise."[55] Although the Greeks adopted the technological use of money, little guidance was given towards monetary philosophy. In fact, the world would have to wait quite some time before the philosophical debate warmed up.

Medieval scholars, such as St. Thomas Aquinas or even Nicole Orseme, the French proponent of the monetary *rentiers* (those who had accumulated large pools of wealth and continued to profit and expand such wealth by using their capital to derive interest income payments through financing trade and issuing loans), focused the bulk of their monetary musings to examining "Aristotle's condemnation of lending at interest as unnatural," or *usury*.[56] Indeed, a great deal of historical monetary debate has been focused on the ethics of usury rather than the actual architecture of the monetary system itself.

Niall Ferguson reminds us that the term "banking" stems from the *Banchieri*, named for the benches where Venetian Jews changed money or issued loans.[57] The trade of money found a calling within the Jewish religion due in no small part to the fact that Judaism permitted lending money at interest whereas Christianity strictly forbade it. Thus, from the Greeks to the Venetians, little consideration was paid to monetary philosophy; rather all eyes were on whether or not money should be lent to one another at interest.

The issuance of loans remained a necessary but taboo activity isolated to minority groups until an up-and-coming Italian family—the Medicis—found a loophole in the religious understanding of monetary mechanisms. Slowly the trade of lending was allowed to enter the mainstream populace. Before the Medicis, the prevailing politics of religion concentrated the lending industry within specific religious and cultural minorities and indirectly isolated these groups within the larger population for what would become centuries of fear, resentment, contempt, and hostility. The innovation of Giovanni di Bicci de Medici was the creation of a bank that did not charge interest but, instead, charged a small fee for exchanging one currency for another (a large component of European transactions due to the overwhelming variations in regional currencies). In labeling the fee-for-service as an exchange fee rather than an interest expense, the Medici bank was able to fulfill a profitable service in high demand while staying in religious compliance. However, despite finding a way to operate, banking remained a highly scrutinized business with considerable risk. Felix Martin summarizes the banking conditions exquisitely:

> There were the ominous lessons of the potential macroeconomic risks associated with large-scale banking contained in ancient texts like Tacitus' [the Roman Historian's] account of the Tiberian financial crisis. Above all, there were the sovereigns' interest in ensuring the continuing priority of their money, and hence their seigniorage. As a result, the new invention of banking was subjected to draconian regulation. When in 1321 the authorities in

Venice discovered that merchants were practicing fractional reserve banking—holding only a small proportion of their assets in coin of the state—they passed a law specifying that banks must be able to meet all requests for withdrawals in coin within three days. In the same year the Catalonian authorities revised their 1300 order that failed bankers be forced to live on bread and water alone until all their clients were reimbursed. Henceforth, any banker who failed to meet his clients' demands was to be publicly denounced—and then summarily beheaded in front of his bank. It was no idle threat, as the hapless Barcelona banker Francesch Castello discovered in 1360. Under such uncompromising regulatory regimes, domestic banking really was a risky business.[58]

The above passage packs quite a punch in emphasizing the attention banking received through the ages and belies humanity's long-term familiarity with a phrase all too common in recent years—*credit crisis*, with the reference to the writings of Tacitus.

Martin is referring to the Roman historian's depiction of the world's first recorded credit crisis in AD 33 with the crackdown by Emperor Tiberius on an excessive boom in private lending. After reviewing existing statutes—those put on the books by none other than Julius Caesar, which wisely limited total amounts of private lending to wealthy aristocrats—it was agreed that legislation was clear enough, but enforcement had been lacking.[59] As with any monetary authority throughout the ages, once a bubble was spotted and a sufficient desire to pop it occurred, the result was inevitable. As the letter of Julius Caesar's law regarding private lending was duly enforced, chaos ensued as it was embarrassingly revealed that much of the Senate was in breach of the law and "overdrawn." Naturally, the real estate market collapsed, bankruptcies ensued, and a full-scale credit crisis emerged. Although intentions were sound, the result was a financial crisis of a magnitude in which the Imperial Treasury had to fashion a bailout. This bailout extended interest-free loans to intentionally overvalued real estate for a period of three years, triggering happy words from the Senate stating, "Credit was thus restored, and gradually private lending resumed."[60]

It is clear from even a brief review of historical economic conditions that the human story has included complex credit systems throughout the ages and that the narrative of economic development progressing from barter to coinage to credit is woefully inadequate. The previous passage also introduces the concept of fractional reserve banking, the de facto standard of modern central banks, as one that was punishable by death. The severe repercussions of illiquidity for those in the banking profession highlight the risks and anxieties inherent in a monetary scheme in which "faith" in the system is required. Those currently within the profession who are concerned about the excessive regulation of the banking industry in the modern era would be wise to keep current standards in perspective with those imposed on the industry throughout history.

So then, given all of the apprehension and historical examples of banking risks and panics, why did the banking system continue to develop? The economics required for trade are difficult forces to eliminate, even under the penalty of death. Merchants, the public, and even the sovereign were economic participants with certain needs and desires that required transactions with others and inevitably a method to transact. Thus, the conditions of evolving society required economic activity, which, in turn, requires banking and exchange. Although it is highly possible to organize society in a non-monetary system, one in which tribute is paid such as that of the ancient Greeks as described in Homer's *Odyssey* and *Iliad*, or one in which spoils are communal as illustrated by the tribal societies of the Native Americans, the overwhelming momentum of social evolution has favored monetary society on our planet. It remains to be seen if this choice of social organization is indeed the "correct" one or even close to "ideal"; it is, however, the most common form of social organization at the time of this writing and necessitates an understanding of the components of monetary society and of, most importantly, whom controls the power within such a form of organization.

—

CHAPTER 7

MONEY: SOCIAL CONVENTION OR TOOL FOR SOVEREIGN POWER?

Following the collapse of the Roman Empire, the bulk of Europe entered the Dark Ages. The overall monetary system also contracted during this time and did not begin to resume the credit-based system until the Medici's revived banking in the fifteenth century.

Although a great deal of monetary sophistication dissipated as Europe entered the Dark Ages following the decline of the Roman Empire and credit system, the monetary work of early Greek philosophers such as Aristotle survived. In his work *Politics*, Aristotle laid out what essentially became the foundation of Western monetary society that "for the purposes of barter men made a mutual compact to give and accept some substance of such a sort as, being itself a useful commodity, was useful to handle in use for everyday life, iron, for instance, silver, and other metals."[61]

Aristotle laid out a concept of money that utilized a commodity-based form of exchange that had dual values, one inherent in its value as a commodity and one assigned to it as the medium of exchange. Although this dual nature of metal-based money has been inferred from Aristotle and passed down through the ages, Graeber points out that, in fact, "Aristotle had argued that gold and silver had no intrinsic value in themselves, and that money therefore was just a social convention, invented by human communities to facilitate exchange."[62] Clearly, there was confusion, even from Aristotle himself. The uncertainty of exactly what money "is" has vexed monetary theorists since its creation.

The uncertainty of exactly what money "is" has vexed monetary theorists since its creation.

As discussed earlier in these pages, although the Greeks are used as the starting point for money for historians, their philosophical contributions to monetary philosophy were far from fully fleshed out. In later centuries, as the Western world emerged from the Dark Ages, the social engineers turned back to the great philosophers of Greece for guidance regarding monetary thought, and commodity-based coinage quickly emerged as the dominant form of money. By this time in Western civilization, gold and silver coinage had been around long enough to be a meaningful part of an individual's understanding of money and thus the confusion between the social convention versus the commodity value of metal coinage became deeply rooted in the minds of the time. Despite the birth of a philosophical debate of money's "true value" that literally continues to this day, money itself was a tremendous financial innovation— indeed, the first great fintech.

Aristotle's monetary framework, far from the only conceivable one and different from what we use today, was held intact for centuries in Western culture and differed meaningfully from what was being developed elsewhere.

Contrary to modern Western-centric belief systems, there was an exceptionally enlightened philosophic debate of monetary policy occurring in contemporary China. In the fourth century BC, Duke Huan of Qi was lord of one of the four most powerful states in China. Dissatisfied with the limited guidance on more challenging aspects of rule provided by traditional Chinese thought as conveyed by Confucius and Mozi, Duke Huan invited the brightest scholars to join a new academy, the Jixia.[63] Much like a modern think tank, the Jixia was tasked with developing innovative strategies and philosophies of governance to assist rulers in organizing and governing society to ensure longevity and dominance.

The monetary works of the Jixia viewed money in a much different light than that of Aristotle and Western philosophers. The Jixia viewed money as a tool to be used by the sovereign to influence economic activity and social order/control, whereas Western thought imbued money as a natural commodity agreed upon by all parties to use for transactions but hardly a tool for economic or social power for the sovereign. This remained a distinguishing factor between Eastern and Western monetary philosophy for centuries.

CHAPTER 8

WHAT SHALL BE USED AS MONEY AND WHO CONTROLS IT?

Most economic participants understand that the sovereign power—the king or government—of the land dictates what shall be termed as legal tender for exchange within that sovereign territory. In ages past, the mechanism for trade was whatever means the participants agreed upon. The sovereign of a territory, nation, or state could largely control what was used as money by deeming that item as an acceptable payment of taxes or legal tender.

Today, the world runs on fiat money, but this is a relatively new chapter in economic life. As G. Edward Griffin points out:

> The American Heritage Dictionary defines fiat money as 'paper money decreed legal tender, not backed by gold or silver.' The two characteristics of fiat money, therefore, are (1) it does not represent anything of intrinsic value and (2) it is decreed legal tender. Legal tender simply means that there is a law requiring everyone to accept the currency in

commerce. The two always go together because, since money really is worthless, it soon would be rejected by the public in favor of a more reliable medium of exchange, such as gold or silver coin. Thus, when governments issue fiat money, they always declare it to be legal tender under pain of fine or imprisonment. The only way a government can exchange its worthless paper money for tangible goods and services is to give citizens no choice.[64]

Although Griffin is a harsh and unforgiving critic of the world's current embracement of fiat currency, he and others who share his beliefs make compelling arguments about the tremendous risks such a monetary system presents—namely, that fiat currency leads to inflation or a reduction in the value of the currency over time as more and more "unbacked" currency is introduced into the system. The era of fiat currency is a relatively new one. Indeed, the world itself had maintained some form of linkage to gold or silver all the way up to 1971 when President Nixon finally cut the tether to precious metals. Since that date, the world has been floating in a sea of fiat currency. What are the implications of this new environment and is it a good or bad thing? This is precisely the question this text aims to address next.

It is important to note that to fully understand the monetary development that has come to rule the world, we must trace the Western use of coinage and its subsequent evolutions. To be sure, there is a rich and deep history of money beyond the Western story. Griffin himself attributes the architecture of fiat currency to China, stating:

The first notable use of this practice was recorded by Marco Polo during his travels to China in the thirteenth century.

The famous explorer gives us this account:

'The Emperor's mint then is in this same City of Cambaluc, and the way it is wrought is such that you might say he hath the Secret of Alchemy in perfection, and you would be right! . . .

What they take is a certain fine white bast or skin which lies between the wood of the tree and the thick outer bark, and this they make into something resembling sheets of paper, but black. When these sheets have been prepared, they are cut up into pieces of different sizes. The smallest of these sizes is worth a half tornesel... There is also a kind worth one Bezant of gold, and others of three Bezants, and so up to ten.

All these pieces of paper are issued with as much solemnity and authority as if they were of pure gold or silver; and on every piece, a variety of officials, whose duty it is, have to write their names and to put their seals. And when all is prepared duly, the chief officer deputed by the Kaan smears the Seal entrusted to him with vermilion stamped upon it in red; the money is then authentic. Anyone forging it would be punished with death. And the Kaan causes every year to be made such a vast quantity of this money, which costs him nothing, that it must equal in amount all the treasures in the world.

With these pieces of paper, made as I have described, he causes all payments on his own account to be made, and he makes them to pass current universally over all his Kingdoms... And nobody, however important he may think himself, dares to refuse them on pain of death. And indeed everybody takes them readily."[65]

Sufficient study of the great Khan's fiat currency is beyond the scope of this limited text. I would suggest that similar themes may be found in the evolution of money from both an Eastern and Western perspective; however, the destination remains the same. Today, we live in a truly global monetary society with all economic actors participating in the same economic framework, albeit with varying paths that led here and certainly varying future intentions. Some potential future paths may or may not lead to an abandonment of the current system in favor of a cryptocurrency regime built on the burgeoning technology of blockchain. But we will table that idea for the moment and focus instead on how we got to our existing paradigm.

For the purpose of our analysis, we will focus on the evolution of money from coinage, through the various global reserve currencies, to the gold standard, and ultimately to the creation of central banks and their fiat currency regime. I will take special care not to utilize my hindsight bias to judge our course through monetary evolution but instead present the story as it unfolded and offer ideas that may help investors manage our current paradigm and potentially navigate emerging conditions.

CHAPTER 9

FROM BULLION TO COINAGE TO BANKING

When Moses climbed Mount Sinai to receive the Word from God, God gave him a lot more to do than just transmit the Ten Commandments and many associated rules and obligations. God also issued precise directions for the construction of a sanctuary where the Jews were to worship Him, together with a tabernacle to go inside the sanctuary. God began right off by specifying that "thou shalt overlay it with pure gold, within and without shalt thou overlay it, and shalt make upon it a crown of gold round about." That is just the beginning: God even ordered that the furniture, fixtures, and all the decorative items such as cherubs were to be covered in pure gold. The instructions, as they appear in Chapters 25–28 of Exodus, persevere for some eighty paragraphs of painstakingly detailed measurements and designs.[66]

—Peter L. Bernstein, *The Power of Gold*

I t is no small wonder how gold, clearly good enough for the gods, came to play such a large role in human monetary history. But consider that gold itself carries little usefulness to humans other than to create beautiful objects or to be used as money. Too soft to be useful as an industrial metal and too heavy to be easily maneuvered, gold is a peculiar metal, to say the least. Gold is itself simple, a metal that is chemically inert; it is both malleable and imperishable, refusing to mix with any other metal, its radiance lasting forever.[67] Gold has been found on every continent on the planet and is thus universally known across most of humanity. All the gold ever mined still exists somewhere on the planet in beautiful art forms or in the form of bars stacked deep within central bank vaults.

Few physical objects have motivated humans to endeavor more ambitious activities than gold. Gold has motivated both the noblest of human endeavors and the worst acts of atrocity the human mind can fathom. Perhaps our love affair with gold stems from the beauty of its untarnishing luster or from how long its story has been intertwined with our own. The Egyptians have prized gold for millennia, reserving the metal for the gods and the pharaohs alone. As Peter L. Bernstein tells us, "The use of gold in Egypt was a royal prerogative, unavailable to anyone but the pharaohs. That constraint facilitated the way that the pharaohs assumed god-like roles and authenticated their heavenly character by adorning themselves with the same substance that embellished their gods."[68]

Although reserved for use only amongst the elite, the ancient Egyptians did not hold gold only for adornment and hoarding; they also used it to transact large sums of value amongst each other or with outside sovereigns. Whether to settle accounts, pay taxes, or pay tribute, the ancients used bullion (blocks of solid gold) to move large forms of value from one to another. Bernstein reports that when the Queen of Sheba paid tribute to Solomon, she brought some three tons of gold to him.[69] Indeed, up until the introduction of coinage, the primary conveyance of gold was in statue or artifact form or that of bullion.

Until the age of Croesus, gold had brought power and wealth to the elites but pain and often death to the masses. To supply the Egyptian pharaohs with the needed supply, gold had to be mined. The vast majority of gold at the time came from Nubia where it was mined under brutal conditions that later informed many artists' interpretations of what hell looks like and prompted King Ferdinand of Spain, in 1511, to utter "Get gold, humanely if possible, but at all hazards—get gold."[70] The notion that the value of gold had replaced the value of human rights was cemented in Ferdinand's words. How exactly did we get to that point?

Coinage and Inflation, Hand in Hand Since the Beginning

It was the revolutionary introduction of coinage that changed humanity's relationship with gold by ultimately introducing it to the common citizen. Coinage allowed gold to escape the control of the elites, increasing both its utility and its value. The struggle to once again retain control of gold and remove it from the masses is an underpinning of the fintech innovations that came to follow. The remarkable innovation of Croesus, in what is today Turkey, both changed the role of gold and liberalized its ownership.

As we have discussed, the process of utilizing coinage, and thus a monetary society for Western civilization, began in the seventh century BC in Lydia and quickly spread to Greece and then throughout Europe. The coinage used became increasingly standardized over time with specific metals, weights, and stamps or engravings indicating the appropriate economic value and under whose authority such value was assigned. The sovereigns enjoyed the rise of coinage as it enabled storage beyond the capacity of other commodities whose usable value, or economic benefit, degraded with time.

"Money" as we understand it today has many of its origins in this metallic coinage. We can relate to several characteristics of the initial forms of commodity money, in that it was: 1) Scarce, 2) Recognizable, 3) Divisible, 4) Fungible, and 5) Portable.

The 2014 documentary *The Rise and Rise of Bitcoin* states:

> As early economic participants soon learned, the use of metallic coins satisfied these characteristics effectively well. So well, that over time coins replaced most other forms of money except in times of specie (coinage) shortages. With the rise of coinage came the creation of a new locus of power, the issuer of the coins. The issuer of coins was most often the sovereign power and the issuance of coins created a central authority over the money supply, creating a link between the sovereign power and money. The responsibility for the money supply turned out to be an overwhelmingly powerful tool with the capacity to propel a sovereign to greatness or ruin. Predictable and steady management of the minting of coinage created rising economic activity and global acceptance of one's money. Consider that the Wu-shu coin in China held its value for 500 years, while Constantine's Soldarus held its value for over 700 years.[71]

However, within this emerging system of sovereign-controlled coinage, there was a problem. When the sovereign needed more funds and was unwilling to increase taxes, they could simply devalue the coinage, a process known as debasement or seigniorage. Seigniorage played a large role in consolidating the power of the sovereign and limiting that of merchants. As a merchant accumulated wealth through wise business and thrifty industry, the sovereign retained the ability to instantly revalue the store of wealth merchants accumulated without recourse. Dr. Elgin Groseclose described the sovereignties of history as having a "capacity or incapacity for moral restraint in handling that which has been entrusted to them."[72]

When the sovereign needed more funds and was unwilling to increase taxes, they could simply devalue the coinage, a process known as debasement or seigniorage.

Moreover, within a society that had standardized coinage with assigned values, economic participants could cut small parts off a coin and expect it to still carry the same economic value. When conducted on a large scale, coin clipping could result in having enough coin fragments to produce a new coin and thus enrich those willing to engage. In fact, throughout history, both of these phenomena have occurred on a rampant scale leading to an ever-present suspicion of suspect-looking coins and sovereign-led recoinages. Some sovereigns were more willing to engage in debasement than others. At one point in France, coins were debased every twenty months for two hundred years.[73] It did not take long for the global population to identify patterns of monetary management. Monetary regimes that were predictable with steady management of the monetary supply were held in high regard and their coins were accepted without question, perhaps even coveted. Whereas, repeat offenders of debasement found their coins accepted only at discounted prices or, worse, refused altogether. Ironically, the condition of transacting in a discounted coin tended to encourage the sovereign to debase further in a futile and never-ending effort to get "caught up" or solvent.

How can we define the peculiar tendency of the population to recognize and adjust to varying monetary policies? In a word— inflation, the unseen force that erodes the value of money over time. At the same time that coinage created a central authority over the money supply, it also created an invisible "check" on the tendencies of those in control of that money supply.

Inflation can be defined as the gradual increase in prices as a result of more and more pieces of currency chasing a finite amount of goods or services. Miraculously, economic participants can almost sense increases in the money supply and continually adjust their prices accordingly. From an analytical point of view, inflation is perhaps one of the most fascinating components of the financial system. It is explicitly controlled by no one and yet affects everyone. However, it took more than a few centuries before monetary scholars were able to correctly identify what was occurring.

Indeed, history's greatest example of unknowing inflation was that of the Spanish Crown. After discovering a literal mountain of silver in their South American colonies, Spain began substantial annual imports of vast quantities of silver into Spain and thence into Europe. Despite refraining from any debasement, recoinage, or revaluation of their currency, the Spanish coinage began a prolonged decline in value. It was not manipulation of the coinage standard or quality; it was the simple continual introduction of more and more silver into the money supply. The Spaniards were literally drowning in silver. Whereas the Spanish Crown had thought its money problems were over with the discovery in the new world and were the envy of all of Europe, they struggled to pay off their debts with continually cheaper and cheaper money.

But, for the rest of the world, Spain's silver woes were also a blessing. Given Spain's ample supply of silver, there was no need to adjust the coins in circulation. Thus, the Spanish silver currency such as the Spanish silver dollar remained consistent in weight and quality. The Spanish silver dollar, consisting of 387 grains of pure silver, was divided into "pieces of eight" each carrying a value of one-eighth of a dollar.[74] Soon, the Spanish pieces of eight were the standard to which all other silver coinage was compared, and this foreign currency served as the primary currency in the early American colonies.

The long-term effect of varying monetary strategies resulted in creating what would in today's terms be referred to as "reserve" currencies. Coins managed by a disciplined monetary authority, whose debasement or clipping was punishable by the highest penalty and such penalties were routinely and publicly handed out, tended to become so favored that those in possession of wealth held these coins in reserve to preserve their wealth and transacted business or "spent" the far weaker coins. This natural process of selecting quality coinage over debased coinage led Sir Thomas Gresham, an English financier during the Tudor dynasty who lived from 1519 to 1579, to restate Nicolaus Copernicus' earlier observation that debased coinage circulates freely while superior coins tend to disappear from circulation. Murray N. Rothbard describes it thus:

> When government compulsorily overvalues one money
> and undervalues another, the undervalued money will leave
> the country or disappear into hoards, while the overvalued

money will flood into circulation. Hence, the popular catchphrase of Gresham's Law: "Bad money drives out good." But the important point to note is that the triumph of "bad" money is the result, *not* of perverse free-market competition, but of government using the compulsory legal tender power to privilege one money above another.[75]

Consider for a moment that in 1964, the United States Mint issued the last regular circulating nickels, dimes, quarters, and half dollars containing 90 percent silver content. In 1965, would you the common consumer rather pay for an item costing one dollar with older coins containing 90 percent silver content or newly issued coins containing no precious metal whatsoever given that both coins will be "credited" the same exact value? This is precisely why the pre-1965 coins quickly disappeared from circulation and can only be found today in safes, vaults, and vintage coin conventions.

Why did you and I both choose to pay with the base metal coins rather than the silver? It is because, despite the nominal equal value, we internally recognize that precious metals have "value" and automatically overvalue coinage that has both legal tender value but also has precious metal value. Whether this is flawed thinking or the manifestation of a behavioral bias, as discussed earlier in this book, the result is the same. Our perceived differences in valuation dictate our actions and the Gresham-Copernicus law comes into effect. I myself have within my safe bags of pre-1964 coins. For what purpose? It is hard to say. Perhaps I am hedging other assets by holding precious metal, perhaps I am a nostalgic collector of historical money, or perhaps I am a "prepper" waiting to transact in the postapocalyptic society after the next great crash.

Banking's Renaissance

Despite the inherent weaknesses of a coinage-based monetary system, the Western world continued to embrace the use of coins as money, with few alternatives. Merchants and economic participants were faced with a difficult system in which amassing financial assets was not enough to get ahead, given that the value of those assets could be arbitrarily reset. Merchants desperately needed to create a check on the power of the sovereign and the cheating of the clippers, in which excessive devaluing would be kept to a minimum.

Surprisingly, the concept of a different system of exchange was laid out in the explanation of how trade was conducted at a provincial French fair in the early seventeenth century. The 1604 history of the Lyons Fair by Claude de Rubys described another fintech innovation, a marvelous process in which "tens of millions of pounds' worth of business was being done, with the sovereign's money almost nowhere to be seen. The great merchant houses of Europe had rediscovered the art of banking—how to produce and manage private money on an industrial scale"[76] Monsieur De Rubys described how economic participants could attend the Lyons Fair equipped not with burdensome coinage, but instead with paper notes issued by widely known and reputable merchant houses that served as a symbol of value for the assigned owner. The individual could then transfer ownership or assign the bill of exchange to another individual who could then redeem the bill of exchange at the issuing merchant house for the stated value in coinage. More importantly, these bills of exchange could be converted across currencies (for a modest fee, of course) should the new owner live in a different country, province, or state. In order to truly appreciate the allure of bills of exchange written on merchant houses over the use of coinage, one must understand the difficulty of transacting long-distance trade at the time.

The Lyons Fair was not like a fair, as many of today's readers would imagine. The Lyons Fair was a central marketplace for a wide variety of goods used in business. From lumber to peacock feathers, the fair offered a single location to transact across a wide variety of valuable commodities of the day. In order to attend the fair, merchants from all over Europe would travel a great distance. Transporting large amounts of coinage presented an additional risk to fairgoers. The use of bills of exchange dramatically lowered the difficulty of travel to the fair. Indeed, the Lyons Fair provided the renaissance of a credit-based monetary system in the modern era, a tool that proved immensely important and powerful for merchants. No longer were merchants held captive to using only the sovereign's coinage as a means to transact business, and no longer were merchants as preoccupied with concerns over marketplace coin clipping and government-sanctioned seigniorage as a drain on their profit.

Although the newly found ease and effectiveness of bills of exchange issued by merchant houses was a reasonable alternative to the trap of sovereign coinage and seigniorage, the merchants knew that there were natural limits to bills of exchange. In fact, the value of a bill of exchange rested solely on the reputation of the issuing merchant house. Much like modern banking, if the populace feared the solvency of a merchant house, the bill of exchange was virtually worthless. Merchants knew that only the sovereign had the ability to demand acceptance of a single currency. However, as the size of the merchant houses grew, they enjoyed a greater reputation and note-issuing capacity. This led to increasing complexity of their business and expansion into new geographies, which, in turn, promoted additional awareness within the marketplace of the names of the venerable institutions. A system of IOUs or credit-based money went mainstream and in Felix Martin's words:

The private trade credit of even the humblest local merchant, in other words, could break its parochial bounds and, endorsed by a cosmopolitan mercantile name, become good to settle payments on the other side of Europe, where its original issuer and his business were entirely unknown. It was here—in the creation of a private payments system—that the invention of modern banking originated.[77]

Naturally, as the power and influence of merchant banks increased, it was a loss of power to the sovereign. This, of course, did not sit well in most cases, and thus a power struggled ensued. Given that the control over a nation's money is one of the most important and lucrative sources of sovereign power, a disruption to this power, in the form of an alternative system of payments, compromises the central authority of the sovereign and poses a legitimate threat in the revolutionary spirit. As private money and credit through the merchant houses grew, so did the idea that monetary policy was less a right, or whim, of the sovereign and was, in fact, more firmly rooted in the public interest and the needs of trade. Moreover, the merchant houses had created an alternative system of payments should the sovereign fail to adhere to prudent monetary policy and one with international reach, thus extending beyond the sovereign's jurisdiction.

As the power and influence of merchant banks increased, it was a loss of power to the sovereign. This, of course, did not sit well.

The rise of an alternative private system of payments may have constituted a threat to the sovereign, but the merchant banks did not seek to displace the sovereign entirely. Rather, the merchant banks sought only stability of financial asset prices and elimination of seigniorage and coin clippage. The growth of the alternative payments systems placed some necessary restraint on sovereign debasement of the monetary supply and reintroduced the all-important concept of creditworthiness rather than supply of precious metal as the basis for the extension of notes. As Martin points out:

> The great merchant houses had discovered a means of producing an international money beyond any one sovereign's jurisdiction. Moreover, so tightly knit was this cosmopolitan elite, and so expertly constructed its hierarchy of credit networks, that it had no need of precious metal to serve as collateral for it promises to pay. Its money was invisible, intangible, consisting only of the confidence of the small group of exchange-bankers at the tip of the pyramid in one another's abilities to assess risks, to be able to meet payments as they came due, and to limit the issuance of credit.[78]

In the mid-sixteenth century, the monetary system of Europe struggled to find a monetary equilibrium. With the competing powers of the sovereigns on one hand and the merchant houses on the other, and with the increasing role currency and securities markets began to play in setting regional and continental prices on specific goods and assets, England found itself reeling from the outside pressures. The last years of Henry the Eighth's reign created multiple financial disasters for England and in reaction to the poor financial decisions of the

English Crown, traders in Antwerp sold the English pound sterling in such rapid fashion that it declined 50 percent in seven years.[79] Indeed, Henry the Eighth of England should be almost as famous for clipping his country's coins as for chopping off his wives' heads. Despite inheriting a vast fortune from his father Henry the Seventh, and after confiscating the church's assets, he still found himself in such need of currency that he ordered an epic debasement of the currency. From 1542 to 1547 (on into the reign of Edward the Sixth) the pound lost "83 percent of its silver content during this period."[80]

Despite debasement, the resulting decline of the English pound was a very real problem for the Crown, as it increased the expense of all goods purchased in foreign exchanges and dramatically increased the carrying costs of the Crown's foreign debt. The English government had become an excessive debtor in Antwerp, and movements against the currency were proportionate increases in the real burden of those debts. The English Crown was advised by the great Sir Thomas Gresham, founder under will of Gresham's College in London in 1597, as a financier-in-chief, on the creation of a stability fund to intervene in the currency markets (a methodology that would become commonplace within the twentieth century).[81] Sadly, Gresham's insights were well before his time and the Crown resorted to a more conventional action—commandeering the foreign currency reserves of English merchants at Antwerp and declaring them forced loans to the Crown (an action used repeatedly by sovereigns across Europe), thus raising the capital required to cover the obligations of the Crown but doing so within the context of an implicit default of the sovereign.

As Carmen Reinhart and Kenneth Rogoff painstakingly point out in their incredible work *This Time Is Different: Eight Centuries of Financial Folly*, over eight hundred years of data show that sovereigns default on their debt more often than not. In fact, the era of sovereigns actually making good on their financial obligations and borrowing sprees is a relatively new phenomenon. Reinhart and Rogoff contend that sovereigns maintain startling similarities throughout history tracing themes all the way back to Dionysius in the fourth century BC noting:

1. Inflation has long been the weapon of choice of default on domestic debt and, where possible, international debt.
2. Governments can be extremely creative in engineering defaults.
3. Sovereigns have coercive power over their subjects that help them orchestrate defaults on domestic debt "smoothly" that is not generally possible with international debt. Even in modern times, many countries have enforced severe penalties on those violating restrictions on capital accounts and currency.
4. Governments engage in massive money expansion, in part because they can thereby gain a seigniorage tax on real money balances (by inflating down the value of citizens' currency and issuing more to meet demand). But they also want to reduce, or even wipe out, the real value of public debts outstanding.[82]

Reinhart and Rogoff show that inflation and default are nothing new to government monetary policy; only the tools have changed. The transition from metallic to paper currency shows technological innovation but does not create new types of crises. The technological advance of money has only served to exacerbate the effects of age-old financial crises, much like technology has made warfare more and more deadly.[83]

Their book title speaks to this reality, as it's based on words of wisdom from Sir John Templeton, who notably said, to paraphrase:

"'This time is different' are among the most costly four words in market history."

Although the English Crown solved the immediate financial crises that stemmed from currency traders selling the English pound as a protest of the government's reckless borrowing, the result of the implicit default was not lost on the regional bankers, and England's creditworthiness declined further. A new world was dawning, one in which the financial decisions made by sovereign governments were watched and acted on by financial market participants and merchant banks.

The Great Monetary Settlement

Quickly, the world was divided into nations that were credit-worthy and those that were not. Much like today, many governments found their spending needs were often greater than their revenues and they had to result to borrowing. When governments needed to borrow funds, the sovereign "reaped what it had sowed" and found punitive interest payments for those that had a bad reputation managing national accounts. Indeed, the incessant borrowing needs of the sovereigns of Europe is what fueled the growth of the nascent bond market into the creature that James Carville, political advisor to President Clinton, famously described when he said, "I used to think that if there was reincarnation, I wanted to come back as the president or the pope or as a .400 baseball hitter. But now I would like to come back as the bond market. You can intimidate everybody."[84]

As one can imagine, the kings of Europe were not especially pleased when traders, a mere rabble in the streets, determined *if* the King was able to borrow and *at what price*. The merchant banks and the market of traders, brokers, and investors that they created had garnered a great deal of power—so much so that the Scotsman James Steuart, in his 1767 *Inquiry into the Principles of Political Economy*, noted the shift of power in the monetary debate from money being fully under the control of the sovereign to the opposite in that monetary society was "the most effective bridle ever was invented against the folly of despotism."[85]

Monetary society was "the most effective bridle ever was invented against the folly of despotism."

Despite the claims of an innovative new throttle to the inflationary whims of debasing sovereigns laid out by Steuart, the sovereign still retained a great deal of power. Economic participants ultimately conducted transactions based on the coinage of one of the primary economic powers of Europe, and the sovereigns retained full control over the tangible money supply and could, with a stroke of the pen, change the denomination of the coinage (or reduce the weight specifications) and thus debase the currency. Although the merchant banks transacted in an alternative form of payment, any domestic adjustment to a currency had a very real effect on existing contracts often to the detriment of the issuing bank. Moreover, the power of merchant bank credit was fickle, to say the least. Liquidity could evaporate in an instant if the public at large deemed an institution unable to pay. Regardless of how long or carefully crafted the image of a merchant bank, one rumor could cause a run and ruin the most venerable of institutions overnight.

To those who are less familiar with the concept of a "run on the bank," they need not look too far in common culture to find prime examples. In the classic holiday film *It's a Wonderful Life*, the main character George Bailey stops his honeymoon short to prevent a run on his family's savings and loan company. In the great movie *Mary Poppins*, the children unwittingly cause a "run on the bank" during a benign visit to their fathers' place of employment. In short, a run on the bank is when too many depositors request to withdraw their deposits at once. The bank is unable to satisfy all of the redemptions as they have, in turn, loaned out many of the deposits. In essence, banks make their "living" by synchronizing deposits coming in with loans going out, thus few banks ever have the capital required to immediately pay all depositors their funds on request. When deposit withdrawal demand is too high and cash on hand (or reserves) runs low, the bank is unable to meet its obligations and must close its doors to any additional withdrawal requests. The fear of being one of the depositors that are too late to receive funds is what motivates individuals to "run" to the bank and withdraw as much as they can while they can. The erosion of trust, a required component in banking, can occur rapidly and sometimes without cause, resulting in a panic. In many cases, bank panics have ultimately only been resolved when the sovereign steps in to backstop the bank's obligations, otherwise known as a bailout.

Thus, a stalemate occurred in the monetary powers of the time—the sovereigns needed the merchant banks to grant approving credit ratings in order to raise capital and the merchant banks needed the sovereign to refrain from abrupt currency devaluations. In 1697, the two competing interests found a way to both achieve their goals and share power over the monetary system. In a time when many proponents offered varying ideas to solve the funding woes of England after the enhanced indebtedness incurred when William D'Orange ascended the throne and promptly increased military spending to protect the Netherlands (his preceding seat of power as stadtholder), it was the idea of William Paterson's that ultimately took root. Paterson proposed the creation of a bank that would be both privately owned but sanctioned by the sovereign to issue banknotes and later government bonds, thus a public-private partnership. Although it was not the first central bank or national bank, the Bank of England was uniquely successful in satisfying the needs of both the private money interest (the merchant bankers) and the lending needs of the Crown and thus became known as what Felix Martin calls "The Great Monetary Settlement."

Thus, a stalemate occurred in the monetary powers of the time—the sovereigns needed the merchant banks to grant approving credit ratings in order to raise capital and the merchant banks needed the sovereign to refrain from abrupt currency devaluations.

The bank was sanctioned by the Crown and controlled by private bankers, but it assisted the sovereign by effectively raising the credit rating of the British Crown. The involvement of private bankers in the governance of the bank lent an air of credibility and restraint. The monetary settlement was a success: the Crown found greater access to the credit markets at more favorable rates and the private bankers were able to exercise greater control over the threat of debasement, seigniorage, and inflation. The agreement to fund the king, albeit on terms that the directors of the bank would have a statutory say in designing, allowed the private money interests a monopoly in money creation and, by extension, the authority of the Crown.

The bankers lent the king their credit; he, in turn, lent them his authority—and the Bank of England directors had found the philosopher's stone of money.[86] Martin likens the central bank to the coveted philosopher's stone, which is the mythical element that enables Alchemists to turn lead into gold and an object so coveted through the ages that it was rumored to have consumed much of Sir Isaac Newton's time and research.

> **The bankers lent the king their credit; he, in turn, lent them his authority—and the Bank of England directors had found the philosopher's stone of money.**

The invention of central banking was, however, not a mythical object imbued with magic powers; it was instead a technological invention, a financial tool born in the fertile environment of the Enlightenment on the stomping grounds of the Royal Society of Natural Philosophers, and the period's greatest fintech. Indeed, Great Britain entered a period of blossoming economic prosperity. The power struggle for the control of money appeared for the moment resolved. There was, however, one last philosophic struggle yet to resolve—one that once again involved the nature of money itself.

CHAPTER 10

THE QUESTION OF RECOINAGE AND THE VANISHING SILVER

lthough the Great Monetary Settlement and the innovation of the Central Bank would serve to have as much impact on the world as the invention of money itself, there remained some structural issues with coinage. These issues were severe and long-lasting enough that their peculiar traits challenged early monetary theorists and central banks alike. Indeed, the legacy of these coinage questions lingered well into the tweintieth century and plays no small role in the current money revolution underway!

Despite the breakthrough that the fintech innovation of coinage introduced to society and economic activity, there were challenges to its wide-scale deployment that bedeviled even the cleverest governors. Since the initial innovation of coinage, various metals have served as money. With silver and gold as the most popular metals across the monetary landscape, there became issues with regards to obtaining enough of the metals to build a suitable monetary base. This issue most often resulted in the adoption of a bimetallic system in which the monetary base carried both gold and silver coins. It is worth noting that the adoption of bimetallism appears through the lens of history to be the harbinger of doom for a coinage system.

> **Indeed, the legacy of these coinage questions lingered well into the twentieth century and plays no small role in the current money revolution underway!**

Even the strongest advocates of a metal-based currency will comfortably note that only one metal can serve as the legal tender official coinage. The other can be used to assist in transactions but *only* at free-floating market prices. Unfortunately, history is littered with the repeated attempts of governments, in need of additional supply, introducing a secondary metal and fixing by law a fixed exchange ratio between the two. This has always led to disaster. Inevitably, market forces begin to materialize, and once more the Gresham-Copernicus law kicks in, and one of the metals disappears from circulation.

But rather than taking my word for it, let us look at the curious case of Great Britain's vanishing silver.

Before enjoying the lucrative benefits of the Great Monetary Settlement, the British economy had to first reconcile an age-old question regarding money itself: how do we handle the annoying changes in gold and silver pricing in the country's money supply? Less than two years after the creation of the Bank of England, Parliament turned its attention to a heated discussion about the coinage in 1696. The issue at hand was how to address the fluctuations in the market price of bullion. If the market price of silver increased above the stated value of British coins, coins would be melted down and exported in the form of bullion and thus the money supply within the economy would decline. Imagine for a moment the difficulties engaging in economic activity when one cannot seem to get their hands on money itself. If one was so lucky to obtain coinage, it was undoubtedly clipped and worn. Still, it would be hoarded nonetheless for specie had become so dear. By 1695, a government sampling of the money supply indicated that the coins in circulation contained roughly half of the original silver content present when the coins were minted, the effect of which being that silver coins were worth approximately 25 percent more as bullion than coins.[87]

To answer the coinage dilemma, Parliament turned to William Lowndes, then secretary of the Treasury. Lowndes was a longtime veteran of financial markets and known to be an intellectual of English monetary history. Lowndes noted that the issue of coinage had plagued the nation throughout the Middle Ages, as from time to time the value of sterling declined or, in other words, there had been inflation.[88] Although Lowndes was unable to accurately determine the reasons contributing to the inflation, he correctly noted the phenomenon's presence and subsequently recommended to Parliament that the coinage should be devalued. Lowndes made a formal recommendation that the silver coinage should be reduced by 20 percent to bring the coins back in line with the bullion price. This recommendation seemed logical, had historical precedent, and would have mitigated the immediate problem, assuming the silver price remained stable for a period of time. Regardless of logic or long-term economic health, the prospect of a formal devaluation of the coinage was never a palatable process and such ideas had many enemies.

To offer a fair and balanced approach to the recoinage proposal, Parliament invited a leading theorist and now famous proponent of the new constitutional government, the chosen defender of democratic principles, none other than the philosopher John Locke, to weigh in. Locke, of *tabula rasa* fame and the "Father of Liberalism," was not a fan of the idea of devaluation, to say the least. He held that the value of Great Britain's coinage should not change from what Sir Thomas Gresham put down almost a century and a half prior.[89]

In December 1695, Locke wrote a scathing denouncement of the devaluation as well as the philosophical idea behind it. Locke attacked the concept of money itself, asserting that Lowndes and his ilk were attempting to pull the wool over the eyes of the public by suggesting that money was anything other than silver itself. Indeed, John Locke followed the trail set before him by natural law theorists and thus railed against the notion that either the sovereign or the money interests could arbitrarily state the value of a coin. Instead, Locke insisted that the value of coins rested on the commodity base of the metal, not the stamp or declarative value prescribed by the authorities. Locke dismissed Lowndes's notion of coinage value having any relation to the authority of the state, but instead said it was a natural phenomenon. Locke declared that the notion of silver gaining or losing value, independently of the silver content of the coin, was nonsense and that what was happening to the country's coinage was simply the illegal clipping of the coins and that any loss in value was due to the absence of silver. Locke approached the subject as if the monetary authorities had confused the cause and effect. Instead of coins being melted down for bullion because bullion was worth more than the coin, the coins were worth less because someone had clipped them. Locke reasoned that the issue was so large at that point in time because criminal coin clipping activity was occurring on a scale that was previously unimaginable.

It is of little surprise that John Locke and his compatriots would adopt this line of thinking. He and his fellow theorists had only recently accomplished political success in limiting the rights or privileges of the king, after having battled for three decades for political liberalism and constitutional government. Locke was locked into a mental political framework that simply could not yield the potentially unlimited power that accompanies monetary authority. Locke had to wrest power away from the central government and monarchy and instead imbue the silver metal itself with full monetary authority. Thus, money was as much a natural right as were those natural political rights; property rights of the individual existed by nature, not at the whim of any sovereign.[90]

Although Locke was one of the most famous philosophers of his day, his views on monetary policy were outside the norm. William Lowndes and his colleagues had wrestled precisely with this subject throughout their careers to the point that their contentions regarding the value of money seemed quite innocuous. The staunch objection of John Locke caught them off guard and, more alarmingly, also captured the imaginations of the public. Locke's concept of monetary value was more easily understood and adopted by the population and Locke's framework won the day.

Instead of devaluing the currency, Locke suggested that the mint call in all coins and "top them off" to the appropriate level of silver. The result was a great fleecing of the British coffers as the mint called in 4.7 million pounds in silver yet when melted down only had enough bullion to mint 2.5 million pounds at the full official weight.[91] The result of Locke's logic caused a tremendous loss to the Crown, riots in the streets from the ill-informed, and a special bond issuance by the government to help absorb the financial fallout. Felix Martin aptly describes the results of Locke's plan, saying, "Deflation set in: prices fell, business confidence collapsed, and trade contracted."[92]

It is difficult to gauge how surprising this turn of events was for the economic authorities of the time. The recoinage issue should have been a nonstarter, for, according to Martin, "the monetary standard had always been flexible: indeed, that was precisely what the perennial struggle between the sovereign and his mercantile subjects had always been about."[93] The limited monetary philosophy handed down from the Greeks offered this notion of a flexible currency in the name of money itself, "nomisma," "something sanctioned by current or established usage or custom."[94] Martin continues to summarize the monetary guidance passed down through the generations:

> In the *Republic*, Plato called it "a symbol that exists for the sake of exchange." His pupil Aristotle held the same view, arguing that "it exists not by nature but by convention, and it is in our power to change it and make it useless." . . . In the hands of the medieval schoolmen, there even developed a more extreme position—the idea that the convention in question is a deliberate artifact of the sovereign. Monetary exchange, Aquinas said, "was invented by reason, not by nature." It was the "one thing by which everything should be measured . . . not by its nature, but because it has been made a measure by men." As such, it served at the pleasure of the relevant authorities, and "if the king or the community so decides, it loses its value."[95]

It is important to understand the long-lasting effects of John Locke's interlude in monetary theory. A hero to many for his contributions to political liberalism and constitutional government, Locke deserves all of the fame that history has given him. However, the effects of his brief foray into monetary policy not only brought immediate economic calamity to Great Britain but also continue to affect monetary society to this day.

Long after Locke's passing, the theoretical framework he introduced to monetary debates is alive and well in modern society. Locke's gift to monetary metal was a natural value beyond that which can be assigned by man. This notion of gold and silver as having a natural value led to a global economy unquestioningly anchored to metal-based currency and what became known as the gold standard for two and a half centuries after his debate with Lowndes.

Three-quarters of a century after the abandonment of the gold standard by the United States, large sections of the population clamor for the return to such a standard. Notions of "end the fed," "audit the fed," and "no more fiat currency" are all sentiments that at their root call for "real money," a fixed currency, i.e. a return to the gold standard.

It is worth noting that the cry for "real money" or a fixed monetary base is not without merit. Indeed, a monetary base defined by a single metal exhibits an exceptional constraint on inflation. We have noted the damaging long-term effect inflation can have on wealth as well as our general tendency as humans to discount those effects in our financial decision-making. However, that restraint on inflation can also serve as a restraint on economic activity, or, worse, it can pervert intentions of governments, businesses, and individuals away from value creation to a single-minded obsession with the barbarous relic itself. History is not without lessons of those who pursued gold above all else and suffered the full consequences of its riches. From the famed Perseus and later Jason who led his Argonauts in pursuit of the Golden Fleece, to Crassus who drowned in the molten metal, to the infamous Midas and his golden touch, there have been countless stories handed down through the ages to temper our fever for gold. Bernstein prepares readers for his epic story of the human love affair with gold in his book *The Power of Gold* with the following story:

> About one hundred years ago, John Ruskin told the story of a man who boarded a ship carrying his entire wealth in a large bag of gold coins. A terrible storm came up a few days into the voyage and the alarm went off to abandon ship. Strapping the bag around his waist, the man went up on deck, jumped overboard, and promptly sank to the bottom of the sea. Asks Ruskin: "Now, as he was sinking, had he the gold? Or had the gold had him?"[96]

Before we move on to discuss the dangers of propositions to return to a metal standard, we must first take a brief glimpse of the gold standard itself and the economic consequences of allegiance to the shiny yellow metal.

CHAPTER 11

THE GOLD STANDARD

What exactly is the gold standard? Obviously, it relates to gold as the underpinning asset that money is built upon. Yet, the notion of the gold standard remains a hotly debated topic. Make no mistake, there is a population of economic participants around the world that seek a return to the gold standard or even a silver standard in an effort to restore "real value" to money and mitigate the potentially devastating effects of inflation. More than anything, the core issue at play here is that a large portion of economic participants are losing faith in governments or monetary regimes to effectively restrain themselves from printing money to solve massive global debt problems.

Murray Rothbard in his book *A History of Money and Banking in the United States* tells us:

> The nineteenth-century monetary system has been referred to as the "classical" gold standard. It has become fashionable among economists to denigrate that system as only existent in the last decades of the nineteenth century, and as simply a form of pound sterling standard, since London was the great financial center during this period. This disparagement

of gold, however, is faulty and misleading. It is true that London was the major financial center in that period, but the world was scarcely on a pound standard. Active competition from other financial centers—Berlin, Paris, Amsterdam, Brussels, New York—ensured that gold was truly the only standard money throughout the world. Furthermore, to stress only the few decades before 1914 as the age of the gold standard ignores the fact that gold and silver have been the world's two monetary metals from time immemorial. Countries shifted to and from freely fluctuating parallel gold and silver standards, in attempts, self-defeating in the long run, to fix the rate of exchange between the two metals ("bimetallism"). The fact that countries stampeded from silver and toward gold monometallism in the late nineteenth century should not obscure the fact that gold and silver, for centuries, were the world's moneys, and that previous paper money experiments (the longest during the Napoleonic Wars) were considered to be both ephemeral and disastrously inflationary. Specie standards, whether gold or silver, have been virtually coextensive with the history of civilization."[97]

Rothbard suggests that since the creation of coinage itself, we have more or less been on a gold (or silver) standard. For the purposes of monetary analysis, the chapter title "gold standard" refers to much of the late nineteenth century up to the eve of World War I. The gold standard was a period of time in which the governments of the developed world tied the value of their paper currency to gold reserves held by their treasuries or central banks. As Rothbard explains:

In the classical gold standard, every nation's currency was defined as a unit of weight of gold, and therefore the paper currency was redeemable by its issuer (the government or its central bank) in the defined weight of gold coin. While gold bullion, in the form of large bars, was used for international payment, gold coin was used in everyday transactions by the general public. For obvious reasons, it is the inherent tendency of every money-issuer to create as much money as it can get away with, but governments or central banks were, on the gold standard, restricted in their issue of paper or bank deposits by the iron necessity of immediate redemption in gold, and particularly in gold coin on demand.[98]

How then did we get into this gold standard? As it turns out, a man who was once hit on the head by an apple had a little something to do with it. At the turn of the eighteenth century, Sir Isaac Newton turned his attention away from alchemy as he began a new career as "Master of the Mint" for Great Britain in 1696. The use of silver and gold coinage as the primary currency of the realm placed a constraint on commerce, namely that as wealth was accumulated by an individual, enterprise, or foreign agent, the usable money supply was decreased as coins found their way into strongboxes and vaults. Moreover, should the price of the underlying metal rise beyond the stated value of the sovereign, the metal would be spirited away to higher-value uses. In order to maintain an adequate supply of coinage within the economy, something had to be done to reverse the peculiar market characteristics. Thus, it was under the keen eye of none other than Sir Isaac Newton that England entered a period of monetary discipline, determined to maintain an impeccable coinage.

Newton was attracted to the role of Master of the Mint due to his notorious interest in the alchemical arts. Alchemy, or the esoteric brotherhood as it has been known, was that pseudoscience that had bedeviled many great thinkers throughout human history. From DaVinci to Newton, the pursuit of alchemical secrets that were said to have been lost with King Solomon haunted those who fell under its spell, and at the heart of its mysteries was gold. English economist John Maynard Keynes remarked of Newton: "In the eighteenth century and since, Newton came to be thought of as the first and greatest of the modern age of science . . . one who taught us to think on the lines of cold and untinctured reason. I do not see him in this light. . . ."[99] Instead, Keynes viewed Newton as "the last of the magicians, the last of the Babylonians and Sumerians . . . the last wonder-child to whom the Magi could do sincere and appropriate homage."[100]

In more ways than one, Newton was a man of the scientific revolution, but his alchemical fetish kept one of his legs firmly rooted in the twilight of the magicians of antiquity. At the intersection of alchemy and the scientific revolution, Sir Isaac began the great recoinage. Despite Newton's affinity for the mystic arts of alchemy, he approached the efforts of the mint in a methodical and exacting way. Overseeing the first coinage in history that relied heavily on mechanization, Newton oversaw arguably the most efficient coinage process to date. Peter Bernstein notes, "[Newton] was on the scene when work began at four a.m. and when the night shift took over, six days a week. He studied the entire process in great detail and continuously discovered methods to accelerate the output of coins."[101] Exactly what Newton was busy producing was also of note. Owing to the lack of silver and perhaps connected to his alchemical tendencies, Newton's primary product from his time at the mint was the English guinea.

The guinea was the first coin to be produced entirely by mechanized methods, and as we shall see it changed the course of monetary history. Peter Bernstein describes the pivotal coin as:

> . . . a substantial piece of gold—at about eight grams, or a quarter of an ounce, it weighed more than twice as much as a genoin or florin of the thirteenth century. Appropriately enough, the guinea was stamped with a little elephant, the sign of the Africa Company. The edges were inscribed with a motto that read *Decus et Tutamen,* or Ornament and Safeguard, which is believed to have come from a clasp on the purse of Cardinal Richelieu. . . . New issues of silver coins manufactured by these methods soon followed after the appearance of the guinea.[102]

So how did the minting of the gold guinea change financial history? It inserted gold as a primary metal in the growing international monetary system and eventually replaced silver as the centerpiece of the metal-based monetary system. Although silver had been used throughout history as a primary monetary base and at the close of the seventeenth century was the de facto world reserve currency in the form of the Spanish pieces of eight, the significant lack of silver specie in the English economy led to greater attention paid to the production of gold guineas. This occurred at a time of rising economic and military power for England, and as England went, so did the world.

As George Gilder argues in his book *Life After Google*, Newton's most undervalued contribution to civilization was his role in ushering in a new era of money.

Newton's modern critics fail to appreciate how his alchemical endeavors yielded crucial knowledge for his defense of the gold-based pound. All wealth is the product of knowledge. Matter is conserved; progress consists of learning how to use it. Newton's knowledge, embodied in his system of the world, was what most critically differentiated the long millennia of economic doldrums that preceded him from the three hundred years of miraculous growth since his death. The failure of his alchemy gave him—and the world—precious knowledge that no rival state or private bank, wielding whatever philosopher's stone, would succeed in making a better money. For two hundred years, beginning with Newton's appointment to the Royal Mint in 1696, the pound, based on the chemical irreversibility of gold, was a stable and reliable monetary Polaris.[103]

Newton's understanding of the dynamics surrounding the informational power money could provide, namely predictability across time and space, provided him an unwavering discipline with which he maintained England's monetary unit. Milton Friedman shared similar observations some two hundred and fifty years later: money is built on trust, trust that others will perceive a similar value as you do with respect to accepting your money, which is paramount to its role in our society.

It is no surprise then that England's power was waxing while Spain's was simultaneously waning. Indeed, Spain's military power and overseas holdings of vast silver deposits would suggest an altogether different scenario. Given that the Spanish Crown had a seemingly unlimited supply of silver, their capacity to introduce more and more silver into the market had a funny and unexpected effect. The value of silver began to decline relative to gold (inflation). Despite the continual influx of Spanish treasure, the Spanish Crown found itself continually wanting even more silver as each of their purchases steadily demanded higher and higher quantities for the same goods.

At this same time, there was also significant demand from Asia for silver as it was used less as a monetary tool and more as an actual commodity there. The unique exports of the Orient found high demand in Europe, and slowly the Silk Road became a steady river of silver from west to east. This scenario also helped exacerbate England's lack of adequate specie, with two meaningful results: the first was the overwhelming need and attention to Sir Isaac Newton's coinage of gold and the second was the creation of the Bank of England as a clever mechanism to supply the English Crown with desperately needed credit.

The Paper Money Revolution

While Lowndes and Locke debated recoinage, the newly invented Bank of England attempted to assist the economy by printing paper money in lieu of coins. Although the utilization of banknotes by the Bank of England did subsequently change the world as we know it, they were not the first to formally introduce them. That title goes to the granddaddy of central banks, *Stockholms Banco*, under the leadership of Johan Palmstruch. According to the history of the Riksbank in Sweden:

> Stockholms Banco issued the first real banknotes in Europe. They were a great success, but it all ended in a bank failure. It was Johan Palmstruch, founder of Stockholms Banco, Sweden's first bank, who issued the banknotes. The

background to this was that, in 1660, the central government had started to mint new coins of a lower weight than the older ones. This meant that many depositors wanted their old, heavier coins back, as they had a higher metal value. This led to a bank run. To counteract this, Palmstruch started to issue deposit certificates. This was a security that gave the owner the right to withdraw the deposited amount in coins. The special thing about the deposit certificates, which were called credit notes, was that the bank was no longer dependent on having money deposited to be able to lend. Instead, the new certificates were handed out as loans from the bank. They could be used to purchase anything and so the first banknotes in Europe were invented.[104]

Initially, citizens viewed such currency with some hesitation, but over time the banknotes began to circulate. As paper money began to find a place within Western society, a question emerged regarding how to constrain the bank from printing too many such notes. The answer was to limit note issuance based on the amount of gold or silver bullion the bank had within its vaults, or in reserve. This idea of tethering the issuance of paper money to the hard quantity of bullion within the bank ultimately became known as the gold standard.

As England had higher quantities of gold in circulation and the popularity of the English gold guinea increased in Europe, gold became a primary reserve for the Bank of England. As we shall soon see, the Bank of England revolutionized the monetary system and enabled England to boom into an economic powerhouse over the coming years. The significant expansion of credit and paper money that was issued by the Bank of England was backed by the bank's gold reserves. This ultimately became the model for all those who sought to follow the Bank of England. The gold standard was born and Sir Isaac Newton was a central figure at its birth.

The gold standard was born and Sir Isaac Newton was a central figure at its birth.

Commensurate with her growing power, Great Britain slowly moved closer and closer to the center of global financial activity. Murray Rothbard suggests Great Britain built off the success of its introduction of gold into its currency and the fintech innovation of the Bank of England to move the British paper currency, the pound sterling, into the role of the world's new reserve currency.

As we moved through the eighteenth and nineteenth centuries, more countries followed the lead of Great Britain by creating central banks and issuing paper money. As the twentieth century arrived, the Western world had become deeply integrated into a financial system overseen by central banks with the gold standard as its backbone. Liaquat Ahamed brilliantly summarizes the Western financial world on the eve of the First World War in his book *Lords of Finance: The Bankers Who Broke the World*:

> Gold had been used as a form of currency for millennia. As of 1913, a little over $3 billion, about a quarter of the currency actually circulating around the world, consisted of gold coins, another 15 percent of silver, and the remaining 60 percent of paper money. Gold coinage, however, was only a part, and not the most important part, of the picture.

Most of the monetary gold in the world, almost two-thirds, did not circulate but lay buried deep underground, stacked up in the form of ingots in the vaults of banks. In each country, though every bank held some bullion, the bulk of the nation's gold was concentrated in the vaults of the central bank. This hidden treasure provided the reserves for the banking system, determined the supply of money and credit within the economy, and served as the anchor for the gold standard.

While central banks had been granted the right to issue currency—in effect to print money—in order to ensure that that privilege was not abused, each one of them was required by law to maintain a certain quantity of bullion as backing for its paper money. These regulations varied from country to country.[105]

Although the financial technological invention of paper money significantly improved some of the limitations a strictly coin or metal-based currency had, the adherence to the gold standard maintained a vital limit on money printing and inflation. Anchoring the capacity of the central bank to increase money supply to their ownership of a fixed amount of metal reserves allowed comfort for owners of capital that their purchasing power would not erode into worthlessness. However, because of the reliance on reserve bullion supplies, which remained a relatively fixed quantity, the gold standard prevented the money supply from becoming elastic enough to weather the financial storms that have a tendency to pop up from time to time.

Commentators throughout the Western world noted that because of the interconnectedness of international banking and commerce, it would be impossible for a war to emerge, or last longer than a few months. Indeed, as the fateful shot rang out in Sarajevo on June 28, 1914, the world was convinced that financial interests would prevent the assassination of Archduke Ferdinand and Duchess Sophie from plunging the continent into war. As we all know, however, humans can often act in ways that are contrary to our financial health, and Europe was cast into a horrific conflict.

Ahamed carefully illustrates how, during the First World War and into the interwar period, the gold standard strained financial conditions, limiting money supply in times of tremendous need. Out of necessity, the various participant countries were forced off of the standard to survive, creating spikes in inflation and financial destruction to mirror that of the physical destruction of the war. As the strain eased, a rush for countries to go back onto the standard would create unnecessary financial pain for already fragile economies to such a degree that Sir Winston Churchill remarked that one of his few political regrets was listening to the bankers and putting England back on the gold standard too soon.

The "Metallist Fallacy"

To drive the point further, the tendency for society to rely on gold or silver as a required backing to currency has been responsible for no end of mischief. The great Milton Friedman points out in *Money Mischief* that money works because of sovereign acceptance *and* the fact that:

> Private persons accept these pieces of paper because they are confident that others will. The pieces of green paper have value because everybody thinks they have value. Everybody thinks they have value because in everybody's experience

they have had value— as is equally true for the stone money called fei, mentioned earlier in this text.[106]

Both Milton Friedman and Felix Martin carefully point out a multitude of instances throughout modern history in which this basic trust or confidence in money broke down or where there were periods in which money simply was not available. Examples of these scenarios are easily found in the high inflationary periods in the United States following the revolutionary war, the Russian Revolution of 1918, the Irish bank closures of the 1970s, and, of course, the hyperinflation of Germany in the interwar period. During these times, confidence in money evaporated and its "value" became distorted. As Milton Friedman explains, "When they lose faith [in money], they do not revert to straight barter. No, they adopt substitute currencies. The substitute currencies in most inflations in history have been gold, silver, or copper specie."[107]

It is the fact that metals have been widely used as money as well as the historical tendency for citizens to revert to metallic coins during times of currency crises that have fostered what Milton Friedman refers to as the "metallist" fallacy. Simply stated, it is the confusion with the frequency of use of metal as money, to indicate that money *must* be ultimately backed or redeemable for metal. Money, however, transcends any base material, as it is a social construct, not an absolute fixed item in the universe.

Money, however, transcends any base material, as it is a social construct, not an absolute fixed item in the universe.

Clearly, the financial technology that is money is not actually rooted in any single asset or commodity, but is rather a social construct in which all members of society "trust" that it will be accepted by other economic participants. This is an important point as humans have inappropriately confused the essence of money for centuries and continually find themselves drifting back towards gold or silver as the underlying source of economic value.

Friedman goes on to cite how American cigarettes and Cognac were widely used as currency in Germany following World War II before Ludwig Erhard's 1948 Monetary Reform, clearly indicating that currency does *not* require gold or silver backing to function. Furthermore, Felix Martin points out that during the Irish bank closures of the 1970s, IOUs and alternative credit accounts predominantly replaced money and did so for an extended period of time. These credit accounts were not with banks or financial institutions but were instead held directly with merchants and vendors who, ironically enough, often used an individual's local pub owner as the credit reference for unknown individuals seeking credit.

The "metallist" fallacy allowed for the flourishing notion that the gold standard was the desired state through much of the twentieth century, although efforts to maintain the standard resulted in exacerbating economic weakness and simply made a bad situation worse. As the long-lasting pains of the great war and the Great Depression lingered, they created an interwar environment in Germany that experienced first an unprecedented bout of hyperinflation followed by a debt crisis that allowed for a known lunatic to become increasingly dominant and dangerous in politics. Clearly, the gold standard is not without fault in creating the conditions for the rise of Adolf Hitler. Thus, it can be stated that monetary policy, whether intentional or not, often has powerful social and political effects that can literally alter the course of human history.

It is quite clear that monetary policy plays too large a role in society to relegate the understanding of it to a narrow group of the population. We have witnessed throughout history and this text that it underpins more than just our economic lives. Money, monetary policy, and central banking are like all technological innovations—they have both the power to unleash unprecedented prosperity or soul-crushing poverty and desperation.

Money, monetary policy, and central banking are like all technological innovations—they have both the power to unleash unprecedented prosperity or soul-crushing poverty and desperation.

Today we find ourselves in a world that has long since abandoned the gold standard. Indeed, for the first time in history, we live in a world of fiat currency, meaning that there is nothing backing the value of our money other than the fiat of the government in partnership with the central bank. As we move forward in this text, we will first examine what a central bank is and where they came from, before moving on to a more in-depth analysis of the central bank of the United States—the Federal Reserve.

Clearly, we cannot dismiss the role of gold or silver from the monetary paradigm. After all, practically every central bank, as well as many governments and wealthy families, continue to hold large amounts of them in reserve. Some commentators such as G. Edward Griffin and Murray Rothbard would suggest that governments and central banks have intentionally attempted to demonetize gold and silver. They would point to a systematic effort to teach the world that money is fiat currency and is increasingly found in digital format.

Why then do China and Russia continue to purchase gold at an alarming pace? Why do the International Monetary Fund, the United States, or the Bank for International Settlements in Basel, Switzerland, not sell all of their gold reserves? The answer is that whereas gold is not the *only* form of money, it is neither *not* money. As with all financial questions, the answer is not binary; the best course is rarely one of absolutes. In fact, it is precisely the context of the argument for or against gold that has given rise to the newest fintech, that of cryptocurrency.

Before we delve into the cyber world of cryptocurrency, we must first complete our journey through financial innovations to better understand exactly why cryptocurrencies were created in the first place. In many ways, it can be said that cryptocurrencies are a backlash against the current paradigm, against the total financial dominance of central banks.

It is precisely within the context of the argument for or against gold that has given rise to the newest fintech, that of cryptocurrency.

But before leaving the topic of money itself, let us close with the words of Dr. Elgin Groseclose on the awesome power of money:

> The removal of a bar of gold from the vaults of the Bank of England to a waiting steamship may have more influence upon the output of an assembly line in a Detroit automobile plant than the functioning of a crane which sets a motor upon that line for the waiting workmen. More men may go hungry from a rise in the interest rate than a rise in the price of bread. A bank failure may produce more misery than a plague. A change in the money standard may provoke a revolution. "It may well be doubted," said Macualay, "whether all the misery which had been inflicted on the English nation in a quarter century by bad kings, bad ministers, bad Parliaments, and bad judges was equal to the misery caused by bad crowns and bad shillings."
>
> The stability of the modern world rests upon the stability of its money. Yet nothing is more obvious than the fact that money is not stable, that nowhere is money under control. Biologists may control the growth of microscopic bacteria in a culture; engineers, the power of exploding dynamite; electricians, the radiations in the ether, but no one has succeeded in controlling money. Yet money is, more than anything else, the creation of man, a device of his own making.
>
> The history of civilization, said Alexander Del Mar, is the history of money. We may add that the history of money is the story of man's struggle to control it, to live with it, to bring it to do his tasks. Man lives with money, but so far it has not been a successful union.[108]

With this dated but eloquent description of humankind's relationship with money in mind, we now turn to the dawning of a new era of monetary evolution. Enter the central banks.

CHAPTER 12

A BRIEF HISTORY OF CENTRAL BANKING

hat is a central bank? My favorite definition is offered by none other than Liaquat Ahamed in *Lords of Finance*. Ahamed describes the functions of a central bank and their monetary policy functions aptly:

> Central banks are mysterious institutions, the full details of their inner workings so arcane that very few outsiders, even economists, fully understand them. Boiled down to its essentials, a central bank is a bank that has been granted a monopoly over the issuance of currency. This power gives it the ability to regulate the price of credit—interest rates—and hence to determine how much money flows through the economy.[109]

The great Walter Bagehot outlined the critical functions of central banking in his 1873 work *Lombard Street: A Description of the Money Market*, often considered the textbook for central banking in its critique of The Bank of England.[110] Bagehot was a famed economic commentator for *The Economist* who felt compelled to write his observations on the Bank of England as he witnessed the bank's evolution from a banking institution to the world's foremost central bank. Bagehot noted that although there was never a formal announcement by the British government nor a claim laid by Bank of England officials, the bank had transcended traditional banking, through reserve accumulation as well as explicit and implicit powers, to become the reserve bank of Great Britain. Indeed, the bulk of the nation's banks and merchant houses held their reserves at the Bank of England. When financial concerns led to drawdowns of banking assets, the nation's banks turned to the Bank of England. In an effort to codify the effective activity of the Bank of England, Bagehot said that a "central bank must be the final reserve of the country, the Lender of Last Resort and thus must 'lend freely, on good collateral, and at penalty rates.'"[111]

Just as money itself was an innovative technology that began to shift the world towards a monetary society in ancient Greece, and banking was a technological innovation transforming the accumulation of money into a mechanism for the extension of credit and thus economic growth, central banking was yet another breakthrough technology that allowed for an organized and coordinated influence on the total supply of money and credit within a given economy. Although far from divine and inescapably prone to human error, central banking has become one of the most dominant aspects of modern financial life, with literally the power to create and destroy wealth. So how then did we come to live in a world dominated by central banks? It all started in a Scandinavian country, at the edge of the arctic circle.

As discussed earlier in this text, the financial innovation of "money" revolutionized human interactions and ushered in a new era of markets and economics. Whereas the first great financial technology, or fintech, was the invention of "money," the second great fintech innovation was that of the central bank. Modern readers should be keenly aware that our current financial world is driven in no small part by the central banks of the world. Indeed, a great deal of commentary by leading scholars and market practitioners points to the outsized role central banks have played over the past decade as well as the extreme policy maneuvers they have instituted in efforts to stimulate global growth. Mohamed El-Erian tackled precisely this topic of central bank prevalence in modern markets in his 2016 book *The Only Game in Town: Central Banks, Instability, and Avoiding the Next Collapse*.[112] Arguably El-Erian's work is a must-read book for anyone who shares concerns regarding the level of central bank activity in the modern economy and the potential threat to stability such reliance creates.

But how did we get to this point? In fact, where did these all-powerful institutions come from? Surprisingly, the monetary history of Sweden provides the clues to the birth of the second great financial innovation: the central bank.

CHAPTER 13

THE WORLD'S FIRST CENTRAL BANK

Towards the end of the reign of Johan III in the early 1590s, Sweden had already enjoyed a long history of utilizing coins for commerce. However, between 1590 and 1592, the desire to mint additional coins and introduce them into the money supply exceeded the ready supply of silver, the primary metal of the nation's coinage. The mint introduced copper, by combining it with silver, in an effort to push more coins into the money supply. The result was disastrous. The inflation rate surged to 800 percent as the value of the new coins plummeted, "naturally, everyone wanted to be paid more of these paltry coins."[113] In 1624, the first pure copper coins were minted and copper gained a larger role in the Swedish coinage, ushering in the era of the copper standard in Sweden and encouraging the creation of a Swedish copper monopoly.[114] It was mid-century when a real monetary breakthrough occurred—the creation of the bank.

The world's first central bank emerged, albeit briefly, in none other than Sweden's Stockholms Banco of 1656, under the guidance of Johan Palmstruch. As previously mentioned, in 1661, Johan Palmstruch, the founder of Sweden's first bank, introduced a new financial innovation to better facilitate the management of money by issuing "credit notes," the first real western banknotes. The notes were intended to represent money deposited in the bank and were given strict regulation for their usage. Initially, the notes enjoyed tremendous success and Johan Palmstruch was revered as a genius. Perhaps Johan himself began to believe some of what was said about him, perhaps he had some insight into the potential benefits of fractional reserve banking, or perhaps he simply was a good-hearted man that couldn't say no to those in need. Whatever the case may be, Johan began to issue banknotes beyond the regulated amounts of money on deposit.

The Swedish economy enjoyed a tremendous boost from the economic activity stimulated by the increase in money supply that the introduction of more and more banknotes represented. Eventually, Palmstruch issued too many notes, which were essentially unsecured loans, and confidence in their value waned. Sweden's first bank collapsed and failed, and the heretofore national hero Johan Palmstruch was removed from office and condemned to death. In 1668, a new bank was created under the name the Bank of the Estates of the Realm, or Sveriges Rikes Standers Bank. The new bank assumed all of the banking activities of Sweden and arguably learned the hard lessons of Stockholms Banco and the disgraced Johan Palmstruch. Sveriges Rikes Standers Bank continues to operate today under the shortened name of Sveriges Riksbank, more commonly known as Riksbank, and has laid claim to the title "first central bank in the world."[115]

Understandably, Sweden is not usually the country that comes to mind as having the first central bank. The story of Sweden's first experiment in central banking is critical to a full appreciation of the delicate balance all central bankers must maintain. At the time, the

Stockholms Banco was a modern miracle and an engine of prosperity. Although the bank was a private institution, the king chose the management. Clearly, effective management of a bank is critical to success and the tendency for Johan Palmstruch to overissue banknotes placed the entire economy in jeopardy. In today's economy, almost every country on the planet has a central bank and the vast majority of those banks operate on a fractional reserve system, meaning that the banknotes circulating in the economy are not backed by anything other than the bank's credibility. Indeed, commercial banks and central banks alike only have on hand, or in reserve, a small portion of assets relative to the number of outstanding notes. The question that has been wrestled with since the days of Johan Palmstruch and Stockholms Banco is exactly how much is needed in reserve to maintain credibility and stave off a financial panic?

Despite the perceived intelligence of modern economic scholars, there is not a body, individual, or model that can determine exactly how far a central bank can go with policy.

The critical lesson from the Stockholms Banco remains applicable today. Central bankers are bestowed with tremendous power and must operate within a framework of disciplined operational standards, lest they lend too freely in a genuine desire to help their constituents, country, or international economies. Johan Palmstruch appeared to have an admirable and fully understandable intention to assist those in financial need or distress; however, there remains an unknown limit in every central bank's integrity beyond which confidence is lost and an economic crisis ensues. Unfortunately, the point of no return is different for every bank and every country, and it is simply unknowable. Despite the perceived intelligence of modern economic scholars, there is not a body, individual, or model that can determine exactly how far a central bank can go with policy. We will only know we have gone too far when it is too late!

Although the Riksbank is still in operation today, it was the creation of another central bank that ushered the world into a new era of economic activity and served as the model for a new generation of banks. On a small island, at the center of a growing empire, a cabal of bankers formed The Bank of England and, thus, changed the world forever.

CHAPTER 14

—

THE BANK OF
ENGLAND

T he middle of the seventeenth century was one of tremendous upheaval in Great Britain. Known generally as the English Civil War, the period culminated with the victory of Oliver Cromwell on the side of the English Parliament against the king that solidified Britain's future as a constitutional monarchy. Although Cromwell came and went from the great stage, the story of how a group of bankers changed the world begins shortly thereafter when the revolution of 1688 (otherwise known as the Glorious Revolution) brought William and Mary to the throne. Known more formally as William D'Orange, Prince of Orange, and Stadtholder of Holland, William III, King of England, Ireland, and Scotland, ascended the throne in 1689. The reign of William and Mary brought a period of political stability for the first time in nearly a century.

Although the newfound political stability was a wonderful environment for business, the years of conflict and costly wars had left the Crown and public finances in a dismal state. The coinage of the realm was worn and clipped, and the country experienced several periods where specie could hardly be obtained. At the time, the

Spanish pieces of eight acted as the de facto reserve currency for much of the world, due in no small part to the steady supply of Spanish silver flowing across the Atlantic from the South American Spanish mines in the infamous treasure galleons of the Spanish Armada.

For those who could obtain coinage, the tendency was to hoard it deep in the vaults of the goldsmith bankers. As concern increased regarding both the need for a secure repository of financial assets and an improved methodology for both private and public lending, the country began to evaluate innovative ideas.

One such proposal was the creation of a land bank, in which banknotes would be issued for public trade and would be backed by the land of the realm itself. Obviously, citizens could quickly understand the solvency of such a currency, but the fixed amount of land to serve as collateral placed constraints on this form of currency's capacity for future growth. However, another clever idea began to circulate and started to gain some traction.

Great Britain and the Dutch Republic alike had emerged from underneath the waning power of the Spanish Crown over the prior century. Under the Hapsburg Empire, the Spanish Crown extended tremendous global influence. Both Great Britain and the Dutch Republic were able to gain freedom from Spanish influence albeit in two remarkably different ways. Whereas England had chosen to meet Spain where her power was, namely at sea with warships, the Dutch chose a different tact altogether. While Queen Elizabeth I of England was narrowly defeating the Spanish Armada at sea, the Dutch conducted a much quieter maritime upset.

Focusing their efforts towards mercantilism, the Dutch honed ships with hulls that allowed sailing in shallow waters as well as a seafaring knowledge that became the stuff of legend. The Dutch naval innovations allowed them to quietly amass a fortune in international trade and business connections. Naturally, this financial success led quickly to an accumulation of financial resources that pooled in cities such as Amsterdam. Eager to keep their funds at work, the Dutch merchants revitalized an older profession known as banking as well as introduced a new one through the formation of what became known as the company. Before long, Amsterdam held financial influence well beyond its size, and, in more ways than one, became the envy of other nations eager to see rivers of money flow through their specie-deprived capitals.

Largely inspired by the Dutch example, Scottish entrepreneur William Paterson proposed a new solution to Great Britain's poor financial state and invited the public to invest.[116] Paterson proposed a bank modeled after the Amsterdam Wisselbank, which would become the official banker and debt manager for the government of Great Britain. After quickly raising 1.2 million pounds of private investment, the Bank of England was formed, and its Royal Charter was sealed on July 27, 1694. Although the bank was primarily created to provide a loan to the English Crown of 1.2 million pounds at an interest rate of 8 percent, its role in financial history quickly ballooned into arguably the most influential financial innovation in history.[117]

The bank opened for business in the Mercers' Hall in Cheapside before relocating to the Grocers' Hall in Princes Street. In 1734 the bank acquired property in Threadneedle Street where it slowly grew in size over the following century. Although the bank's early years were focused on assisting the Crown in debt financing and the issuance of new coinage, it gradually opened its doors for conventional banking, deposit taking, and ultimately the issuance of banknotes.[118] At the time that bills of exchange and later banknotes were becoming an accepted form of currency, the recoinage process was being carried out by Sir Isaac Newton. Newton methodically oversaw the recoinage, pressing out golden guineas that began to circulate throughout the British economy and supplant the Spanish pieces of eight. However, the real story was in the increasingly common use of banknotes to settle accounts.

Although the Bank of England was founded in 1694, it took the better part of a century to fully realize its role as the central bank to Great Britain. The bank did not obtain dominance over the issuance of banknotes until 1709, it was not appointed receiver of public money for the state lottery until 1710, and it wasn't until 1760 that it administered more than two-thirds of the national debt.[119] It was not until 1776 that it metamorphosized into a central bank truly deserving of Adam Smith's statement, "The stability of the Bank of England is equal to that of the British government," indicating that without the bank, the government would have lacked creditworthiness and without the British government, the bank would have lacked authority.[120]

Whereas a multitude of banks offered banknotes that could be redeemed by the bearer for a specified amount of gold or silver, the Bank of England banknotes began to carry a premium as they were perceived to be less risky or prone to bank default and had an implied backing from the Crown due to the close association of the two institutions. Indeed, the Bank of England banknotes and their "promise to pay" were considered as good as gold.

It was not until the Bank Charter Act of 1844, some one hundred and fifty years after the bank was founded, that the bank was granted a formal monopoly on issuing notes in England and Wales. Additionally, the legislation ensured that "the Bank of England became the sole monetary authority for the United Kingdom, and this arrangement is still in place today."[121] However, the bank was restricted to only issuing new banknotes when there was a corresponding increase in the bank's gold reserve. Thus, the Bank of England was firmly on the gold standard.

With all of these developments, the Bank of England was not yet a central bank as we define them today. In fact, the bank still thought of itself as a private bank that enjoyed a particularly powerful strategic partnership with the government. However, it was in response to the financial panic caused by the Overend-Gurney crisis of 1866 that the bank began to realize that it had become the reserve bank to all other commercial banks in the country and to some overseas. The bank had finally fully transformed into a central bank. Walter Bagehot's edict of a central bank being the lender of last resort had come to fruition, intentionally or not, and the Bank of England ushered in a new era of finance.

Throughout the twentieth century, the Bank of England has very much grown into its role as a central bank and has been one of the largest contributors to the economic activity of the century. Perhaps the most significant adjustment of policy demonstrated by the bank in the twentieth century was the 1931 abandonment of the gold standard, a move that hinted at the new era of fiat money. Although there have been periods of waxing and waning global economic influence commanded by the bank, it remains a tremendous force in global markets and has served as the model for all the central banks that have followed.

CHAPTER 15

MONEY BY FIAT

"From antiquity until the mid-twentieth century, citizens of even modest means might have some gold or silver coins. Today there are no circulating gold or silver coins."

—James Rickards, *The Road to Ruin*[122]

O ver time, the question of "what is money" has significantly evolved. What served as money moved across assets and commodities. Slowly over the twentieth century, gold and silver vanished from circulation as money and paper currency replaced them. Initially, the paper was redeemable in gold or silver but over time that link was severed. Now the bulk of paper currency in global circulation is something altogether different.

As innovative as the Bank of England was, it was not the pioneer of paper money issued by fiat. The use of items of little worth as a standard for money backed only by the force of a strong ruler has had its moments in history. Cleopatra pioneered the art of using metal coinage that had no intrinsic value within the metals themselves.

Eschewing away from gold and silver, she minted coins of base metals that carried value only because she declared them to. As Stacy Schiff, Pulitzer Prize-winning author of *Cleopatra: A Life*, tells us:

> In economic affairs she took a determined hand, immediately devaluing the currency by a third. She issued no new gold coins and debased the silver, as her father had done shortly before his death. For the most part hers was a bronze age. She instituted large-scale production in that metal, which had been halted for some time. And she ushered in a great innovation: Cleopatra introduced coins of different denominations to Egypt. For the first time the markings determined the value of a coin. Regardless of its weight, it was to be accepted at face value, a great profit to her.[123]

We have seen that the initial utilization of paper currency backed by nothing other than the legal decree of the monarch was that of the Great Khan. However, it is important to note that outside of China, the Khan's money was virtually worthless. As Bernstein points out:

> People demand that their money must have *value*. In fact, valueless money is not even money, because it would not serve as a means of payment and would be nothing that anybody would want to accumulate or consider as wealth. Metallic money, or paper money convertible into metal, is usually considered to have more value than a system that uses paper only. As Ma Twan-lin reminded us, "Paper should never be *money* or produce." The presumption here

is that metals are more limited in supply than paper, which means that metallic systems should prevent money from becoming valueless.[124]

Marco Polo's account of fiat paper money in medieval China notwithstanding, the first attempt at fiat paper currency in Europe was in Sweden but ended quickly in a spectacular failure. The first experiment of truly fiat paper money in the West took place in none other than the pioneering start-up colonies of the soon-to-be-formed United States of America in the period from 1690 to 1764.[125] Differing from Sweden's early example, the colonists had no choice but to issue paper money without an explicit tether or constraint, leading naturally to over-issuance. The colonies resorted to fiat paper money to manage shortages of gold or silver money and the result was a cycle of painful inflation. These early experiences led George Washington to vocalize his thoughts on paper money issued without gold or silver backing. He said, "We may one day become a great commercial and flourishing nation. But if in the pursuit of the means we should unfortunately stumble again on unfunded paper money or any similar species of fraud, we shall assuredly give a fatal stab to our national credit in its infancy."[126]

Washington's comment and the American Colonial experience with fiat currency illustrated a significant component necessary in the process—an independent powerful monetary authority. In antiquity, this authority was the sovereign such as Cleopatra or the Great Khan in Marco Polo's time. However, as society evolved, there began a slow erosion of some of the financial power through chronic mismanagement and strained wartime finances. This transition necessitated a new entity to steward the financial system. The Bank of England was the first successful candidate to grow into this role and largely defined the path for all future followers.

The famed bank at the centerpiece of Felix Martin's "The Great Monetary Settlement," the Bank of England, was the public-private partnership that ushered in the slow establishment of the central banking era. Although the bank began as a private investment interest, it was nationalized in 1946 and then owned in full by the government rather than by private stockholders.

Despite the nationalization of the institution, many conspiracy theories continue to circulate speculation around private ownership and the potential that the bank is essentially a tool of a small group of wealthy elites, most often the Rothschild family, to enslave the citizenry in a web of debt. In fact, such conspiracy theories continue a false narrative associating these same wealthy elites with the likes of Alexander Hamilton and a notion that the central banks of the United States, in their various forms over the years, were and are controlled by these same moneyed interests. These theories, as interesting and imaginative as they are, should be largely dismissed as they can be of little use to us as investors! What is important and useful to investors is the way in which central banks influence markets and execute monetary policy.

In the world of monetary policy, there are two primary opposing forces that push or pull the economy. These competing forces are inflation and deflation. Naturally, inflation is a condition in which more money is chasing the same number of goods and prices rise, whereas deflation is when prices for goods drop. Inflationary and deflationary cycles can persist for long periods of time but one fact is certain: it is far more difficult for a central bank to "manage" deflation than inflation and, thus, central bankers attempt to create a low and consistent inflation rate at all times.

I, like potentially many of you, began my discovery of how central banks worked with shock at the fully intentional effort to systematically *create* consistent inflation within an economy. I was stunned at how the adoption of fiat currency enabled a central bank such an extension of power to inflate. However, after exhaustive historical research into currency, default, debasement, and inflation, I can now appreciate the significant innovation that the Bank of England represents. The Bank was and is the necessary great compromise between the sovereign and the private citizens for a mutually comfortable equilibrium, or a goldilocks level of acceptable price stability, not too hot and not too cold. Keep in mind that the US inflation rate in 1979 was that of 200 percent, making the current Federal Reserve inflation target of 2 percent sound much nicer, indeed.

The Bank was and is the necessary great compromise between the sovereign and the private citizens for a mutually comfortable equilibrium, or a goldilocks level of acceptable price stability.

As the institutions of central banking have evolved over the centuries, they have gathered an air of mystique. Perhaps some of the mystery surrounding central banks is related to the often dry and highly technical nature of finance and monetary policy, but a healthy dose of intentional obfuscation is also present. As Federal Reserve Governor Jerome H. Powell states in his March 28, 2017, speech at the West

Virginia University College of Business and Economics, "Historically, the activities of central banks were shrouded in mystery. Montagu Norman, the famously secretive governor of the Bank of England from 1920 to 1944, reportedly took as his personal motto, 'Never explain, never excuse.'"[127]

By the turn of the twentieth century, the European countries all had fully functioning central banks with the most influence on the continent wielded by the Banque de France, the Reichsbank of Germany, and the Bank of England. The United States was still without a central bank and in most circles of the Western world was considered a financial backwater prone to panics and crises. While the US was a booming economy, it was stifled by credit restraints and liquidity issues in no small part due to the fragmented banking system.

The US was also a country in transition from an agricultural economy to an industrial economy, which placed competing demands on the nation's currency and credit system. The agricultural bulk of the land was in want of credit during planting seasons and flush with cash during harvest. Meanwhile, the growing industrial and commercial centers of the northeast had currency and credit needs whose timeliness did not often synchronize with the agricultural sector. Indeed, these fundamentals helped usher in many of the banking and credit crises within the US, culminating with the Panic of 1907. Playing an equally large role in aggravating credit calamities was the role of the gold standard. The gold standard served as a governor of sorts on the seemingly unlimited money printing capacity of central banks, by limiting each bank by law to specific reserve requirements. At the time, the gold standard served as the constraint that kept the monetary powers "honest," limiting their capacity to print money and thus debase the currency.

The gold standard was, in large part, the only check on the almost limitless power wielded by central banks. However, make no mistake, the monetary authority possessed by the central bankers was unprecedented in human history and only gaining speed. This was not without notice by Americans. The hottest emerging economy of the era, the United States, was becoming too familiar with financial boom and bust cycles, and a growing faction of the financial elite began to desire what Alexander Hamilton had fought for over a century earlier—an American central bank.

Such was the stage at the turn of the twentieth century. The Western world was fully governed by the twin pillars of central banks and the gold standard. The United States was on the verge of joining the Bankers Club, but the ghost of Andrew Jackson maintained a firm grip on the American populace. Americans held a strong apprehension to central authority, especially when it came to money. But before we examine the birth of what has become the world's most powerful central bank, the Federal Reserve, let us conclude this section by revisiting the significance of observing central banks in society.

Neil Irwin sums up the importance of understanding central banking in his book *The Alchemists* with this statement:

> Democratic societies entrust central bankers with vast power, because some things are so important yet technically complex that we can't really put them to a vote. We are wrong to expect perfections, but we must demand progress. The story of central banking is also the story of civilization, discovering in fits and starts how to manage a just society, forever taking small steps to a better world.[128]

It is clear that central banking is a technology that has enabled tremendous growth across the planet and ushered in an era of unprecedented economic transformation. In fact, central banking is now the underlying framework of the entire global financial system.

Again, I am reminded of Niall Ferguson's statement that "financial history is the backbone of all history" and thus a critically important but often overlooked story of the evolution of modern society. I heartily agree with both Irwin and Ferguson and take it a step further, contending that central banking has become the underlying framework on which all economic activity—and, thus, human capacity to survive and thrive in society—is built. Although it has not always done so, the world now lives in a monetary society governed by central bank policy and vulnerable to imperfections in theory as well as policy mistakes—until, of course, a new innovation cuts an altogether different way forward.

In short, the evolution of money is far from over. The next player that we will examine was not the first but has become the most powerful financial player in the world. The world has changed dramatically since its controversial birth in 1913, but the Federal Reserve has come to sit at the center of global finance, earning with its many mysteries the nickname from G. Edward Griffin of "The Creature from Jekyll Island."

SECTION 3

The Federal Reserve

CHAPTER 16

AN INTRODUCTION TO THE FEDERAL RESERVE

There are few financial or governmental institutions that have garnered more suspicion or speculation than the Federal Reserve. Ripe with controversy since its inception, *the Fed,* as we often call it, has been intertwined with conspiracy theories throughout its existence. Eustace Mullins places no finer point on the issue than with the title of his 1954 book *The Federal Reserve Conspiracy*. His text opens with a brief note from the author:

> The birthplace of the Federal Reserve Act, Jekyll Island, is now operated as a public park by the State of Georgia, but the tourist will find no plaque there commemorating the event. This is not so much an oversight on the part of the park officials as it is a triumph for the more than adequate publicists of the Federal Reserve Board, who have perpetuated the comfortable fiction that the Act was born in the halls of Congress, the product of the minds of Carter Glass and Woodrow Wilson. It is the writer's hope

that this and many similar fictions will not long survive the publication of this work.[129]

G. Edward Griffin continued with Mullins' theme with his own text entitled *The Creature from Jekyll Island: A Second Look at the Federal Reserve*.[130] Mullins and Griffin both point out some critical realities to the Federal Reserve, namely that it was designed by a small group of politicians and bankers at what was then J.P. Morgan's club on Jekyll Island and that it is a private/public institution, not a freestanding government agency. Modeled in many ways after the Bank of England and the other European central banks, the institution is a combination of private bank credit and government sovereign monopoly of the money supply.

Naturally, any time there exists a strong concentration of power, and especially when that power relates to money, there will be heightened awareness by the public. Given the extent to which we have discussed the struggle over the concepts of "what is money" and "who controls it" within this text, it should come as no surprise that the concentration of power over the money supply within the individual liberty-loving United States would necessarily come with significant concern. However, conspiracies and speculation aside, the Federal Reserve has transformed over the past century from another example of the power of fintech to arguably the most powerful financial institution on the planet today. For this reason, we shall take a brief journey through the history of the Federal Reserve before continuing on to an examination of the breadth and depth of its influence in the world today.

It is perhaps helpful for those who do not have a firm understanding of what the Federal Reserve is and what it does to offer a brief summary. Established in 1913, the Federal Reserve is the third installment of a central bank in the United States. Created by the 1913 Federal Reserve Act of the U.S. Congress, the Fed (as it is most often known) is charged with the responsibility of controlling the monetary and interest rate policies for the United States; in effect, it is the central bank of the US.

Although the monetary policy efforts of the Fed get the most attention, they are only a fraction of the actual activities at the Fed and its twelve district banks. In fact, 83 percent of the Fed's resources are spent on bank supervision, management of currency, paper-check processing, and electronic payments.[131] It is the smaller 17 percent of Fed resources that get the most coverage, with often global coverage of the activities of the Fed's Federal Open Market Committee (FOMC) meetings and policy announcements.

The FOMC is comprised of the seven board of governors stationed in Washington, D.C., and the twelve presidents of the district banks. The district banks are spread throughout the country in New York, Philadelphia, Boston, Chicago, Cleveland, St. Louis, Kansas City, Richmond, Atlanta, Minneapolis, Dallas, and San Francisco. The FOMC is required to meet only four times per year, but they typically meet every six weeks. It is in these meetings that the Fed sets policy objectives such as the federal funds rate, the rate at which commercial banks loan to each other on an uncollateralized overnight basis.[132]

The Fed is charged with utilizing its power to keep people employed, keep inflation low, and keep interest rates in a moderate range.

In brief, the statutory objectives for monetary policy, as defined by the Federal Reserve Act, are maximum employment, stable prices, and moderate long-term interest rates. In layman's terms, the Fed is charged with utilizing its power to keep people employed, keep inflation low, and keep interest rates in a moderate range. The Federal Reserve is unique among other central banks of the world in that it has multiple objectives (often referred to as its "dual mandate" of maximum employment and inflation control). To achieve these objectives, the Federal Reserve utilizes the discount rate, reserve requirements, and open market operations as its primary tools. The definition of each of these standard tools is described in the chart below:

Policy Tool	Definition
Discount Rate	The rate at which eligible institutions may borrow money from the central bank, typically on a short-term basis, to maintain liquidity during times of internal or external disruptions.
Reserve Requirements	The minimum amount of customer deposits that a commercial bank must hold as reserves (or refrain from lending out).
Open Market Operations	The engagement by a central bank in the open market to buy or sell government bonds, the purpose of which is to exert influence/control over interest rates (primarily short-term interest rates) and the supply of base money in the economy.[133]

Although the primary tools of the Fed are the discount rate, reserve requirements, and open market operations, the central bank is not limited to these activities alone. Within the United States, investors have become all too familiar with the extraordinary measures available to a central bank, with *quantitative easing* becoming a common expression in the nomenclature. Simply stated, when responding to a crisis, if the central bank can no longer reduce interest rates yet feels the need to further expand liquidity, the bank can enter the market and directly purchase long-term bonds in an effort to push the interest rates of those bonds lower. Although rarely discussed prior to the financial crisis of 2007–2008, quantitative easing is in effect an open market operation and functions because the central bank has the authority to bring money in and out of existence.

Fiat money is a necessary core of many modern central banks in that the central bank can increase or decrease the monetary supply based on fiat. In essence, a central bank can create more money by simply willing it into existence. This responsibility for correctly balancing the *appropriate* level of money in an economy is one of the many primary points of contention in the argument for or against central banking.

America has had a contentious relationship with the Fed since its controversial creation. Moving in and out of the American spotlight over the past century, the Fed has understandably become intertwined with a wide range of speculation, fear, mistrust, and policy judgment. It is no wonder that such widespread confusion about the Fed exists when even Fed insiders such as Danielle Booth describes the Fed thus:

> Created after a massive stock market collapse and subsequent bank failures that decimated depositors' savings, the Federal Reserve exists so that the American public can maintain faith in its monetary system. This vital responsibility is carried out by an organization with an arcane, complex, and peculiar decision-making apparatus that is virtually opaque to outsiders.[134]

In many ways, our relationship with central banking predates our country (driven largely by anxiety regarding the Bank of England)

and was most notably expressed in our formative years by the debate between Alexander Hamilton (pro-bank) and Thomas Jefferson (anti-bank). A history ripe for conspiracy theorists, the creation of the Federal Reserve is an interesting story and deserves a few words.

CHAPTER 17

WHAT IS THE FEDERAL RESERVE AND WHERE DID IT COME FROM?

Roger Lowenstein sums up the functions of the Federal Reserve in his fascinating book *America's Bank: The Epic Struggle to Create the Federal Reserve* as follows:

The basic federalist structure enacted a century ago remains in force, so does the essential purpose. Then as now, the Fed serves as a banker to other banks and the keeper of their reserves. Along with setting the short-term interest rates and supervising the banking system the Fed is in charge of the nation's monetary policy. Then as now, the Fed provides liquidity to the system, especially in times of crises, so that banks may supply the country with adequate credit.[135]

The Federal Reserve has not always been in existence in the United States and it is certainly not the first American central bank. The country has had a rocky relationship with the role of a central monetary authority and has, in fact, had three central banks. To better understand the current bank, the Federal Reserve, it is worth examining a brief history of the American central bank experience.

The United States found its nationalistic roots in its freedoms. One of those freedoms that served as a strong underpinning of the revolution itself was one of monetary freedom. Colonists sought protection from taxation without representation, but they also fought a cycle of indebtedness to the monetary authorities of Great Britain. After the Revolution, the fledgling country was free from the financial constraints of the British Crown and the Bank of England, but it was now forced to create its own remedy to the need of managing the government's money and regulating the nation's credit.

One of the nation's first great internal debates emerged between Secretary of the Treasury Alexander Hamilton arguing for the creation of a central bank and Secretary of State Thomas Jefferson arguing against a central government entity in total control of the monetary supply. Thankfully, Lin-Manuel Miranda has brought elements of this famous debate back into the minds of the public through the groundbreaking 2015 musical *Hamilton*.

Eventually, Alexander Hamilton convinced Congress of the financial stability a central bank could provide, and the First Bank of the United States was created in 1791. The First Bank of the United States set the template for all future American central banks as it was created with a capital stock that was both government and private funds, thus creating a quasi-public/private entity. The bank started with $10 million—$2 million being public funds and the remaining $8 million being private ownership. Directors ran the bank, with twenty-five chosen by the government and twenty chosen by the private investors. The First Bank of the United States was created with a twenty-year charter.[136]

Americans themselves stayed as divided as their representatives on the subject of the bank. When the charter came up for renewal in 1811, President James Madison, who himself had originally voted against the bank, could not help persuade enough of Congress to continue to support it and the bank was abolished, albeit in an extremely close contest, failing in both houses by a single vote.[137]

The following period was chaotic as the relative stability the bank provided evaporated immediately. In addition to instability with respect to credit markets, state-chartered banks proliferated, issuing their own varying banknotes. This led to confusing currency restraints in trade and increased bank panic risk, as the redemption capacity of noteholders was always in question.

The strains of the financial markets were compounded by the War of 1812. The Federal government was faced with the increasing costs associated with war, a higher degree of unpredictability in the credit market and in its ability to efficiently issue debt or government securities, and the lack of a safe repository for Federal funds with a reliable mechanism to move those funds from place to place.[138]

In response to the volatile vacuum that replaced the First Bank of the United States, Henry Clay, speaker of the House, introduced a bill to Congress that would charter a Second Bank of the United States in 1816. Ironically enough, Clay himself had opposed the renewal of the First Bank of the United States and when asked about this reversal, he said the following: "The force of circumstance and the lights of experience" had caused him to change his mind.[139] The Second Bank of the United States was similar to the first except in size and makeup. It began with a capital stock of $35 million with one-fifth of the funds coming from the government and one-fifth of the directors appointed by the president.[140]

One of the primary arguments against the First Bank of the United States was whether or not the entity itself was deemed constitutional. This debate was put to rest in the 1819 Supreme Court case of McCulloch v. Maryland, which affirmed the bank's constitutionality. The argument, however, did not end there.

The Second Bank of the United States was quickly seen as so large and powerful that it built on the speculative fears already embedded in the population. Debate of the bank's control over individual financial freedom and business interests raged for the following two decades. During this period, an 1832 bill to recharter the Second Bank of the United States to allow continuance beyond its impending expiration date was vetoed by President Andrew Jackson. The administration's clear antagonism to the bank was much ballyhooed by the political opposition during the 1832 presidential campaign, in an effort to undermine Jackson's popularity. But the natural distaste of the American public with respect to a large central financial authority was widely underestimated and Jackson was reelected in no small part due to his opposition to the bank. When the charter expired in 1836, the Second Bank of the United States ceased to exist. It is said that on his deathbed, when asked of his proudest accomplishment as president, Andrew Jackson stated, "I killed the bank."[141]

It would be seventy-seven years before the United States experimented with central banking again. During those years the financial system of the US was characterized as a series of significant booms and busts. This was an extremely volatile period of chaotic credit markets and monetary supply. State-chartered banks dominated the landscape and banknotes varied wildly. During the Civil War,

President Abraham Lincoln oversaw the passage of the National Banking Act of 1863, which was followed by amendments in 1864 and 1865. This was an attempt to bring some measure of stability to the financial markets and, although helpful, was unable to solve the nation's currency and credit woes. It is, however, interesting to note that some of the National Banking Act's legacy lives on in communities across America today in the names of many prominent local banks. As the National Banking Act was enacted, the banks that chose to participate were incorporated into a national banking system with a level of interconnectedness and note issuance privileges. As banks in a community signed onto the system, they were given the name "National Bank." Thus, in a community, there would be the First National Bank, Second National Bank, and Third National Bank, indicating their order of acceptance into the National Banking System. Although the banking system has evolved substantially since the National Banking Act days, many banks continue to operate with names inherited from the National Banking System.

During the late nineteenth and early twentieth century, the US banking system was highly fragmented with a hodgepodge of currencies and thin confidence at best. It is difficult for anyone of our era to comprehend the banking system of this time period as we have lived our entire lives within the Federal Reserve era. As Roger Lowenstein explains:

In 1858, the United States was an industrializing nation with a banking system stuck in frontier times. As the country put up factories and laid down rails, the tension between its antiquated finances and its smokestack-dotted towns grew ever more acute. Heated battles over "the money question" came to dominate the country's politics, but no matter how unsatisfied the people, any solution that tended toward centralization was, due to the prevailing prejudice, off the table.

America was a monetary Babel with thousands of currencies; each state regulated its own banks and they collectively provided the country's money.[142]

Born from Crisis

It was during the banking crisis of 1907 that many began to see what truly ailed the country. The panic came when so many Americans could still feel the pain of the massive depression of 1893, and although prosperity returned before the end of the decade, the market participants were becoming tired of the boom-bust cycle.

The 1907 crash was truly a banking system failure. The year itself was a period of economic growth in the country, yet despite the boom, it witnessed a financial panic, credit crunch, and a series of bank runs and failures. The simultaneous occurrence of both GDP growth and economic expansion in the face of recessionary catalysts led many minds to the notion that central banking could, in fact, bring stability to financial markets. The goal was to smooth out the negative effects of recessions by adequate monetary policy, thus decreasing the cyclical demands on liquidity related to a predominantly agricultural West and the consistent need for funds in metropolitan finance centers in the East. The financial needs of the country could be solved by a central monetary supply source, and it could provide for consistent growth by solving the liquidity needs and the underlying bank stability problems of the economy.

The banking crisis of 1907 was a self-propelling negative feedback loop—as one bank collapsed, rumors would circulate about even the healthy banks, leading nervous depositors to demand their money. This led to full-scale runs on the bank, which ultimately caused them to fail. The panic was played out in the stock market as well, culminating with the infamous event in which J.P. Morgan coordinated with other bankers to design a plan to save themselves. Once substantial assets reentered the market, asset prices found a floor and began to recover, and the panic subsided. It was not lost on politicians and financiers alike that such a power was dangerous when it was in the hands of a small number of private citizens (especially when those citizens were in the twilight of their life like J.P. Morgan). It was seen that the government needed the same capacity for stabilization that Morgan exhibited in the 1907 panic, and suddenly the difficult work of creating the United States' third central bank took hold.

> **The government needed the same capacity for stabilization that Morgan exhibited in the 1907 panic, and suddenly the difficult work of creating the United States' third central bank took hold.**

The period following the panic of 1907 was the forming ground for what would become the Federal Reserve. The debate leading up to the creation of the third central bank of the US was contentious, to say the least. There was a struggle between the need for a significant and intelligent central authority to solve financial crises and the lingering fear of concentrating power in the hands of bankers, who were seen as highly wealthy individuals bent on furthering their own agendas at the expense of the populace.

Although it is widely known that Senator Nelson Aldrich was an early supporter and initial architect of provisions towards the third central bank in the US, he was simply too politically close to Wall Street and the perceived cult of money to have his name attached to any real legislation regarding such an institution. Instead, Aldrich facilitated the efforts of other figures less politically charged than himself to navigate the critical legislation. Prominent bankers and high-profile government officials largely conducted the planning for the nascent Federal Reserve in secret. This secrecy, no doubt, fueled the fears of the anti-bank faction and sparked many of the conspiracy theories that linger on today.

At the onset of bank planning, there was a train that left New York for Jekyll Island. Onboard were the original architects of what would become the Federal Reserve. The "conspirators" on Senator Nelson Aldrich's midnight train were Arthur Shelton, Aldrich's personal secretary; Frank Vanderlip, president of National City Bank; Professor Piatt Andrew, Assistant Secretary of the Treasury; Paul Warburg of Kuhn, Loeb, & Company; and Harry Davison of J.P. Morgan & Company.

Lowenstein describes the event as follows:

> It was Davison who arranged for the group to stay at Jekyll Island, an exclusive club where J.P. Morgan was a member. The ruse was that they were going duck hunting, and so Warburg, feeling faintly ridiculous, obtained a hunting rifle and cartridges that he had not the slightest idea

how to use. On a frigid night, softened by falling snow, the voyagers, traveling singly and incognito, made their way to the Pennsylvania Station across the Hudson River, where Aldrich's private railcar was attached to the rear of a southbound train. The blinds were drawn, with slivers of amber light marking the window frames. Inside, the car was all polished brass, mahogany, and velvet.[143]

Frankly, how could such a scene not become the stuff of legend and speculation? It is true that Senator Aldrich orchestrated a late-night train ride in 1910, in which the prominent US senator and several other leading Wall Street tycoons departed New York in secret to sequester themselves on Jekyll Island, Georgia, to create a plan for the nation's banking system. However, the secrecy was a necessary evil as Senator Aldrich knew that, should the legislation be traced back to Wall Street, it would be doomed to fail. Regardless, the gentlemen from New York created a central bank framework that balanced the unique concerns of the growing American economy—namely to have concentrated enough monetary powers to be effective yet offer a diverse regional component to adequately represent the varying economic conditions of the country as well as to appear as if the power is not concentrated in New York or Washington, D.C.

Work towards an agreeable system of central banking progressed in fits and starts over the following two years. Whereas Nelson Aldrich had been the initial champion of the bank, it is arguably Paul Warburg who deserves much of the credit as the father of the bank. Warburg, a German banker, came to the United States from Europe where the major countries all had central banks. His status as an outsider allowed him a level of comparison that eluded most Americans of the time.

Lowenstein summarizes it this way: "If Jackson had stood against the supposed evils of centralization, Warburg, more than anyone else, had recognized the weakness in stand-alone banking and crusaded to overcome the Jacksonian view. It was an American prejudice, a parochialism, which he as a foreigner had seen more clearly."[144] Paul Warburg's consistent work finally culminated with the election of a new president.

In 1912, Woodrow Wilson was elected president and immediately set to work on bringing stability and reform to the American financial system. The second major initiative of his presidency was the creation of the Federal Reserve. Working diligently with his Treasury secretary, William McAdoo, to find a compromise between the various concerns regarding the structure of the bank, the final bill was passed by both the House and Senate on December 23, 1913, and was signed into law by President Wilson within hours.[145] Wilson aptly described the significance of the legislation stating, "I cannot say with what deep emotions of gratitude. . . I feel that I have had a part in completing a work which I think will be of lasting benefit to the business of the country."[146]

Wilson could not know at the time the extent of the lasting benefit he had ushered in. The creation of the Federal Reserve enabled the United States to catch up with European countries with respect to banking, and it created the financial infrastructure for the US to gain international financial leadership over the following century. No longer was the US a financial backwater; in fact, the Federal Reserve may have been a bit late to the game, but it would soon become the guiding financial force for the rest of the globe.

The Federal Reserve may have been a bit late to the game, but it would soon become the guiding financial force for the rest of the globe.

Roger Lowenstein effectively summarizes the creation of the Federal Reserve by saying:

> The Federal Reserve Act did not guarantee sound monetary policy any more than the establishment of Congress could guarantee good laws. Policy would be the burden of those in power—as disputatious today as in 1913. However, the Act unified the banking system, which unquestionably made it stronger. It created an institution for regulating the money supply, a difficult task but a necessary one for societies too advanced to depend on the vagaries of mining gold. It provided flexibility to respond to financial shocks and economic headwinds and thus made the system more resilient. It was an imperfect bill—nonetheless, after a decade of debate, division, panic, study, conspiracy, party platforms, elections, and legislative work, it was a highly worthy achievement.[147]

The Four Ages of the Fed

It is worth noting that the age in which the Federal Reserve was born and the age we find ourselves in today are quite different. I would dare say the Fed has lived through four distinct ages over the past one hundred years, beginning with the Gold Standard Age, then the Bretton Woods Age, on to the Fiat Currency Age, and lastly into our current age, the Supranational Central Banking Age.

The Fed was born into the age of the gold standard and found its footing within the paradigm of balancing the economic health of the economy with the quantity of gold held on reserve in its vaults. This balancing act helped foster some of the disconnects between Fed policy and the economic facts bearing out within the US economy leading up to the Great Crash of 1929 and the subsequent depression. Under the leadership of Benjamin Strong, the Fed worked to both manage the US domestic economy and assist the Bank of England in managing UK gold reserves in efforts to protect the global economy should England run out of gold and fall into a deep recession. At the time, Britain's pound sterling was the reserve currency of the world. Issues stemming from a collapse of Britain's economy would have had ripple effects across global markets. To this end, the Fed followed a policy of relatively relaxed monetary standards that helped push the speculation in domestic markets arguably higher than they would have perhaps otherwise been. This period illustrates the challenges presented by a rigid gold standard in that it demands high-interest rates and aggressive gold accumulation (a form of policy tightening) during periods of economic stress, suggesting a compounding of negative pressures for economic participants.

In the aftermath of the Great Depression, the central banks of the world struggled to get back onto the gold standard, which manifested strained financial conditions that largely did not end until the outbreak of World War II (and in many ways contributed to the rise of Hitler in Germany). During the war, all hopes of a gold standard were abandoned as countries borrowed excessively and printed money to finance war efforts. Following the war, a new system of the world was designed by the participants at the Bretton Woods Conference in July of 1944. Some 730 participants from forty-four Allied nations gathered at the Mount Washington Hotel in Bretton Woods, New Hampshire, to create a new basis for international monetary policy. Both the International Bank for Reconstruction and Development and the International Monetary Fund were created at this conference. However, the key component of the conference was the agreement towards a new monetary system that placed the US dollar at the center of global finance.

Rather than each individual country striving to return to the gold standard, they would instead link their constituent currency to the US dollar and the United States would remain on the gold standard, thus becoming the link for all other nations to gold. In essence, the currencies of the world "outsourced" their gold standard to the United States, and the US dollar became the official global reserve currency, ushering in the second age of the Federal Reserve.

In essence, the currencies of the world "outsourced" their gold standard to the United States, and the US dollar became the official global reserve currency, ushering in the second age of the Federal Reserve.

The Bretton Woods Age continued until August 15, 1971, when President Richard Nixon officially closed the gold window. Although it had been illegal for US citizens to own gold since the 1930s, the gold window of the United States was the formal link between all global currencies to the precious metal. When Nixon closed the gold window, he not only took the US off of the gold standard but also took the entire world off of the gold standard. This action formally pushed the world into a purely fiat currency regime in which all of the major currencies of the world were issued by fiat with nothing backing them. The untethering of global currencies from any legitimate backing plunged the world into an inflationary spiral as users of money tried desperately to determine the "value" of their pieces of paper. The Fed found itself in an altogether new age, the Fiat Currency Age in which it had to undergo, under the steadfast leadership of Paul Volker, a series of substantial interest rate hikes to halt the rapid rush of domestic inflation. Since then, the world has been adrift with respect to currency prices. Without any form of backing, the relative value of an individual currency has been transformed into a combination of monetary policy, government fiscal policy, and ultimately "trust."

I would contend that this age of fiat currency ended with the financial crisis of 2007–2008. In the period that followed the creation of the Federal Reserve, the institution itself struggled to find its role in governing the US economy. Learning from its mistakes, especially its monetary policy during what became the Great Depression, the bank evolved the primary methods for regulating liquidity in the markets. Adjusting the interest rate known as the federal funds rate has become the Federal Reserve's first line of defense in managing over-speculation and, on the opposite end of the spectrum, underutilization in the economy. Until the most recent credit crisis and market crash of 2007–2008, it seemed the Fed had become so adept at managing the economy that it was perceived that the days of market crashes and severe recessions were over.

Obviously, we have learned that this is not the case. Investors today must be just as aware of the risks of market declines and damaging recessions. The Federal Reserve has shown exceptional creativity in utilizing experimental monetary policy in the wake of the financial crisis. Many of the innovative methodologies were quickly modeled by other global central banks in an effort to boost economic activity. Despite the progress made since the great recession, the Fed remains a topic of dispute. The primary result of the financial crisis was the breakdown of "trust" in the monetary authorities.

Against a backdrop of expanding policy tools and innovations in economic engineering, there has been a shift in perception of the monetary powers including a reemergence of centuries-old questions about what money is and who controls it. This, I believe, is the fourth age of the Federal Reserve, one in which the Fed and other monetary powers are expanding beyond the confines of traditional central banking and are evolving into supranational central banks against an increasingly leery population of money users.

CHAPTER 18

SUPRANATIONAL CENTRAL BANKS

The fintech innovation of central banking did not end with central banks themselves. In fact, the evolution of money continued past the innovation of banking and central banking into something altogether larger. Over the course of the twentieth century, much of the world embraced a similar form of social organization centered around money. This transition has been most noticeable in China, where top-down communist rule has opened up to allow more market-based financial organizations and activities. The globe has embraced monetary society. Within this global monetary society there arises a need for financial institutions that can transcend national boundaries and, in many cases, a single sovereign authority to facilitate the flow of funds on scales unprecedented in human history.

There has long been a question that circles around banking. If an individual or business runs out of money, they turn to the bank. If the bank runs out of money, they turn to the central bank. What happens when the central bank runs out of money? The initial response in a fiat currency paradigm is that the central bank can simply print more money. This is often a pointless exercise as inflation typically destroys the new funds faster than they can be printed. Instead, the offending country is expected to approach the International Monetary Fund, the Bank for International Settlements, or another reputable third party of largess. Indeed, in the global monetary architecture, these institutions were created or have evolved to be the lender's lender's lender of last resort—they should be supranational central banks.

In many cases, these institutions fulfill their role. The International Monetary Fund (IMF) has been instrumental in assisting countries all over the planet in navigating challenging economic times. Observation suggests that the IMF is typically utilized with emerging economies, and often their assistance comes with prescriptive behavior that was meaningfully absent in many of the ground-zero developed economies that were hardest hit by the financial crisis of 2008. Adam LeBor in his book *Tower of Basel* describes the Bank for International Settlements (BIS) as "the bank for central banks."[148] It is clear that there are international financial institutions that can offer assistance to isolated crises, but what happens when large central actors in the global financial theater are in trouble? Did the IMF or the BIS enter the conversation when the United States and Europe were in the throes of the great recession?

Contrary to the intended architecture and many long years after the financial crisis, it has become evident that the most important player in the global financial game of thrones has been the Federal Reserve. Adam Tooze carefully and exhaustively documented the shift of the Federal Reserve from a central bank to a supranational central bank in his 2018 work *Crashed: How a Decade of Financial Crises Changed the World*. Tooze carefully documents the steps the Fed took to save the global economy through the expansion of its balance sheet:

The Fed was inserting itself into the very mechanisms of the market-based banking model. The relationship between the state, as represented by the central bank, and the financial markets was nakedly revealed. The Fed was not just any branch of government. It was the bankers' bank, and as the crisis intensified, the money market reorganized itself accordingly, taking on the shape of spokes with the Fed as the hub.[149]

Documenting the high usage of international banks of the Fed's discount window, an emergency lending facility typically associated with a negative stigma, Tooze goes on to demonstrate that many of the innovative new funding facilities the Fed created during the crisis such as the Term Auction Facility (TAF), the Primary Dealer Credit Facility (PDCF), and the Commercial Paper Funding Facility were built to assist domestic *and* international constituents. Of the total lending for the TAF program, 51 percent of the borrowing was by international banks.[150]

It was, however, the restoration of a much older facility that really did the trick in preventing extreme euro-dollar or sterling-dollar currency crises from compounding the pain of the financial crisis. Tooze says,

Having gone out of use in the 1970s, the swap lines had been briefly revived in 2001 to deal with the aftermath of 9/11. In 2007 faced with the implosion of the transatlantic banking system, they were repurposed and expanded on a gigantic scale to meet the funding needs not of sovereign states but of Europe's megabanks.[151]

Once limits were reached with respect to directly lending to international financial institutions, the Fed evolved once more to provide nearly unlimited dollars to a select group of foreign central banks that would then extend the dollars to their domestic institutions. The Fed supplied this precious dollar liquidity to the European Central Bank (ECB), the Bank of England, the National Bank of Switzerland, the central banks of Scandinavia, the bank of Japan, and, following on the success of these programs, later extended the facilities to key emerging market central banks: Brazil, Korea, Mexico, and Singapore.[152] When it was all said and done, the Fed had established swap lines with fourteen central banks and floated some $4.45 trillion dollars when standardized into twenty-eight-day terms.[153] Much of this was conducted not so much in secret but instead obfuscated through the infamous dry and technical jargon employed by central bankers. There is little doubt that the Fed played the largest role in arresting the global financial crisis and did so with little public awareness or thanks.

The Fed evolved during this period to reach a new level of central banking the world has never before seen. To be sure, the actions taken by the Fed were not without their rewards, as Tooze explains:

> Every cent of this staggering flow of funds was repaid in full. Indeed, the Fed made profits of c. $4 billion on its swap lending in 2008–2009. But this sober accounting understates the drama of this innovation. Responding to the crisis in an improvised fashion, the Fed had reaffirmed the role of the dollar as the world's reserve currency and established America's central bank as the indispensable central node in the dollar network. Given the even vaster volume of

daily transactions in global financial markets, it is not the sheer size of the effort that mattered. The Fed's programs were decisive because they assured the key players in the global system—both central banks and large multinational banks—that if private funding were to become unexpectedly difficult, there was one actor in the system that would cover marginal imbalances with an unlimited supply of dollar liquidity. That precisely was the role of the global lender of last resort.[154]

The Fed kept these swap lines in place. In 2015, China found itself suddenly experiencing a shortage of dollars that had the capacity to turn into an entirely new crisis. Although Beijing was slow to react, the stimulus efforts introduced were enormous but could not facilitate the creation of dollars needed. Once more the Fed stepped in and provided dollar liquidity through the swap line with the Bank of Korea that had been established during the financial crisis. The result was a tumultuous third quarter in 2015 but not a full-blown crisis, thanks in no small part to the Fed. Like it or not, many of us today are likely solvent primarily because of the actions taken "behind the scenes" of the Federal Reserve.

Like it or not, many of us today are likely solvent primarily because of the actions taken "behind the scenes" of the Federal Reserve.

CHAPTER 19

CENTRAL BANKING CONCLUSIONS

We have seen how the Fed was a relative latecomer in the era of central banking. It was far from the first of these new fintech innovations, but it has become the most powerful. The Fed has survived three prior ages of central banking, each with its own challenges. Since the financial crisis, it has evolved largely out of necessity to become a supranational central bank and has been claimed by some to be the world's central bank.

Although there are plenty who would claim that central banks played a role in getting the global financial system into trouble, there is no doubt that the Federal Reserve was instrumental in preventing the financial crisis from getting meaningfully worse. In many ways, the Fed saved the system as we know it and enabled the rest of us to debate the results today. But at what cost? It is arguable that there exists now substantially more attention, commentary, and distrust of central banking than prior to the crisis. It is into this new era of renewed debate over the role and value central banks create that the Fed, and the global financial system, treads.

Our story does not end here, but it appears to represent the early pages of a new chapter in monetary revolution. We are yet in the nascent years of a new era of central banking and on the cusp of a new generation of fintech that is taking direct aim at the banking and central banking paradigm.

We are yet in the nascent years of a new generation of fintech that is taking direct aim at the banking and central banking paradigm.

There is a growing movement, domestic and abroad. A revitalization of the debate that is as old as money itself. Given the role the Fed has taken on, it could be argued that there has yet to be an institution that has been more successful. Why then could there be critics such as G. Edward Griffin who plainly state:

> We do know that the Federal Reserve System must be abolished. Let us, therefore, begin.
>
> The creature has grown large and powerful since its conception on Jekyll Island. It now roams across every continent and compels the masses to serve it, feed it, obey it, worship it. If it is not slain, it will become our eternal lord and master.
>
> *Can* it be slain? Yes it can.
>
> *How* will it be slain? By piercing it with a million lances of truth.
>
> *Who* will slay it? A million crusaders with determination and courage.

The crusade has already begun.[155]

As you are entertaining these words, there are certainly more than a million crusaders working away on their computers. They most likely did not fall into their current pursuit through considerations of monetary policy. It is likely that they really did not give much thought to the concept before finding their new passion. It is even more likely that they have all found their calling by very different routes. By strange circumstances, interest has given way to a movement—not so much a movement away from central banking but instead a movement towards something new . . . towards cryptocurrency.

SECTION 4

The Rise of Cryptocurrency

CHAPTER 20

THE HISTORY OF MONEY REVISITED

"Bitcoin is an attempt to adapt the advanced computerized system that we have, the internet, to resurrecting what money used to be all about."

—Gene Epstein, The Rise and Rise of Bitcoin[156]

I n 1999, while still in college and not long before I settled into a career in financial markets, I picked up a fictional book about cryptography. Cryptography is the study of codes and, more importantly, code-breaking. The book was titled *Cryptonomicon*, and it was written by Neal Stephenson.[157] Far be it for me to go into the story of the text here, which, although enjoyable to read, is far from the subject matter of this book. It did, however, introduce me to an idea that has come to dominate today's news—cryptocurrency.

As computers have come to revolutionize every facet of our daily lives, it is unreasonable to think that they would not one day intersect with money. Obviously, we are all too familiar with the way in which money has gone digital, with our ubiquitous use of debit cards and online transactions. However, the notion of digital code actually replacing money itself has indeed seemed like science fiction or a dystopian reality until 2018. I will personally mark 2018 as the year cryptocurrencies entered the mainstream—not because Bitcoin (the most widely known cryptocurrency and in many ways the original pioneer) hit $20,000 but because CNBC began to track the value of Bitcoin with as much diligence as it tracks the Dow Jones Industrial Average or the Standard and Poor's 500 indices. Even the venerable Chicago Mercantile Exchange began futures contracts on Bitcoin, which, to many traders, legitimized the space.

As computers have come to revolutionize every facet of our daily lives, it is unreasonable to think that they would not one day intersect with money.

So what then is this thing called Bitcoin and the cryptocurrency revolution? I am glad you asked. Bill Gates called it "a technological tour de force" in the documentary The Rise and Rise of Bitcoin.[158] But before we work towards exactly what cryptocurrency is, let us first revisit some of our prior subject matter to understand why it is. Let us now reimagine the evolution of financial history but purely from the perspective of the user of money, disregarding the interests of sovereigns, bankers, and economies. Dare I say, let us view the world as perhaps a millennial would?

Previously on *Money Revolution*

As we have explored, the innovation of money carried with it tremendous centralized power. Although prior to the creation of coinage gold and silver had been reserved only for the elite, once minted into coins, they underwent a democratization of sorts and quickly became the money of the people. Throughout history, the overwhelming majority of governments were unable to resist the temptation that such power provided and repeatedly debased their currency. The result was intentionally hidden taxation on the citizens that effectively resulted in a wealth transfer from those who could least afford it to the elites. Naturally, this led to a distrust of the ruling class and the money supply.

To combat the devastating effects of debasement and the hidden taxation of inflation, merchant bankers and sovereign powers in need of credit reached a compromise. They devised a scheme in which they would share power over the money supply—the sovereign providing exclusive rights to manage the money supply and the bankers providing credibility that they would do so prudently. Central banks were born and ushered in a new era of financial complexity not without its ups and downs.

Central banks worked diligently to "manage" the money supply, but it proved far too challenging for banks to convince the world that they could refrain from the temptation to debase. Banks were instead restricted by a need to maintain an adequate reserve level of gold to back their paper currencies and the gold standard was born. However, during the First World War, the vast majority of the major banks abandoned the gold standard, forced by the costs of war to print more money than they could back with gold. Despite fits and starts thereafter, the world never truly returned to the gold standard again.

After the Second World War, a new global financial arrangement was made. In the majestic setting of the Bretton Woods Hotel on Mount Washington in New Hampshire, the Bretton Woods Agreement was ironed out. This agreement essentially pegged the major currencies of the world to the dollar rather than to gold, whereas the US dollar was the only currency to be tied to gold. This arrangement removed the need for other central banks to engage in the destructive game of "get gold at all costs," and it allowed them to manage their currencies with more "elasticity" or flexibility. The agreement also ushered in an era of the US dollar as the world's reserve currency. The agreement created supranational financial institutions that would, in a way, serve as central banks to the central banks (i.e., the World Bank and The International Monetary Fund).

However, on August 15, 1971, President Richard Nixon shocked the world by closing the gold window, effectively terminating the redemption of the US dollar into gold. Given that the dollar was the anchor holding the entire global currency system to some form of gold reserves, this move ushered in a new era of money—fiat money. From this point forward, the major global currencies were issued by fiat, backed by nothing, and functioned only on the population's trust in the central bank. Naturally, the 1970s are remembered to this day as a period of high inflation, the type of inflation many people fear repeating. However, given the significance of what had occurred—the essential abandonment of gold as money after thousands of years of use—it is no wonder that the world was sent into an inflation fit.

Only after an aggressive interest rate tightening cycle by Federal Reserve Chairman Paul Volker was inflation in the United States brought seemingly under control in the 1980s. Indeed, as the '80s and '90s came and went and the US entered the 2000s, there seemed to be a sense that the Federal Reserve had finally solved the equation that is the economy. Then the worst financial crises since the Great Depression hit and many people began to question, perhaps for the first time in their lives, who was in control of the money and what was any of it really worth?

People began to question, perhaps for the first time in their lives, who was in control of the money and what was any of it really worth?

Growing up as a child watching your parents struggle to keep their job or their home, or graduating college with substantial student debt and no job prospects on the horizon, or losing your first job with a brand-new wife and baby at home can all affect the way one views the financial system, especially when that system is built on trust. It is not a far stretch to liken the generation that grew up in the financial crisis as too far removed from the Great Depression-era generations.

We have discussed earlier in this text the extent to which money can affect our minds and I suggest that a financial crisis brings with it long-lasting mental stress that is not easily overcome or put in the rearview mirror.

CHAPTER 21

ENTER BITCOIN

Bitcoin has certainly become a buzzword. It represents an entirely new concept that has, in large part, taken on a life of its own. If one were writing a book about Bitcoin, one could hardly make up a more mysterious origin story for the technology—not quite the discovery of alien technology from deep space, but every bit as interesting.

Ben Mezrich, author of *The Accidental Billionaires*,[159] says of Bitcoin:

> I believe that Bitcoin and the technology behind it have the capacity to upend the internet. Just as Facebook was developed to enable social networks to move from the physical world to the virtual one, cryptocurrencies such as Bitcoin were developed for a financial landscape that now functions largely online. Bitcoin may have been a bubble— during last year's cryptocurrency crash, Bitcoin lost nearly a third of its value in just one week—but the technology behind it isn't a fad or a scheme. It's a fundamental paradigm shift, and it will eventually change everything.[160]

So, what exactly is Bitcoin? Technologist George Gilder offers his definition in his book *Life after Google: The Fall of Big Data and the Rise of the Blockchain Economy*:

> *Bitcoin:* A method of secure transactions based on wide publication and decentralization of a ledger across the internet. Current credit card systems, by contrast, are based on secrecy and centralization and use protected networks and fire walled data centers filled with the personal information of the transactors.
>
> Bitcoin's public ledger of transactions is collected in blocks roughly every ten minutes, beginning with the current block and going back to the "Genesis block," created by Satoshi Nakamoto, the pseudonymous inventor of Bitcoin. Each block is confirmed when at least half the participants in the Bitcoin verification process—the "miners"—hash the block mathematically with all the previous blocks since the Genesis block. In order to change or rescind a transaction, therefore, more than half the computers in the system have to agree to recompute and restate all the transactions since Genesis.
>
> Bitcoins are not coins, but metrics or measuring sticks for transactions that are permanently registered in the blockchain.[161]

On Halloween of October 2008, while the global financial markets were in the midst of the greatest meltdown and recession since the Great Depression, an anonymous person, or persons, named Satoshi Nakamoto released a paper titled "Bitcoin: A Peer-to-Peer Electronic

Cash System" on an online cryptography mailing list. Nakamoto then released Version 0.1 of Bitcoin software on Sourceforge on January 9, 2009.[162] Despite its destiny to revolutionize the money conversation, it got off to a slow start. It was not until 2011 that Bitcoin began to get some major media attention and its value started to appreciate rapidly.[163]

According to Nakamoto's revolutionary nine-page paper, Bitcoin is "a purely peer-to-peer version of electronic cash [that] would allow online payments to be sent directly from one party to another without going through a financial institution."[164] Bitcoin was a new currency not tied to any government or central bank and not reliant on banks and financial intermediaries to facilitate the movement of "money" from one person to another.

Nakamoto added an exceptionally interesting characteristic of his new peer-to-peer electronic cash system, one that immediately differentiated it from the current forms of currency on the planet. He made it finite. As George Gilder says:

> Total circulation will be 21,000,000 coins. It'll be distributed to the network nodes when they make blocks, with the amount cut in half every 4 years.
>
> > First 4 years: 10,500,000 coins
> > Next 4 years: 5,250,000 coins
> > Next 4 years: 2,625,000 coins
> > Next 4 years: 1,312,500 coins
> > Etc . . ."[165]

The limited total supply of Bitcoin has led forward-looking monetary observers to compare the token to gold and the role it has served. The inability for any central authority to create new tokens on-demand, or by fiat, harkens to stable currency fans as the modern or updated version of gold. Quickly understood and hailed by those monetary scholars who are also deeply orientated in technology, Bitcoin and the blockchain technology that underlies it have been described by Gilder as a digital form of gold:

> In 31,000 lines of code, Bitcoin exploits a set of complex cryptographic algorithms that supposedly make it "as good as gold." Or maybe even better! Unlike gold, with the burden and glory of engagement in the real world, where it is rooted in the possibly changing time constraints of extraction from deep beneath the earth, Bitcoin is an entirely virtual, digital entity. Bitcoin, for better or for worse, is entirely an artifact of computers.[166]

The limited total supply of Bitcoin has led forward-looking monetary observers to compare the token to gold and the role it has served.

As innovative and disruptive as Bitcoin is, it is this notion of it being entirely an artifact of computers that has led to its slow integration into the awareness of our popular consciousness. Despite the deep interconnectedness of computers into our modern lives, few of us actually understand programming and the "what" and "how" of computer functioning. Indeed, many of us utilize computers on a daily basis and yet maintain a constant lack of trust with our modern tools. Perhaps we fear what we do not understand, or more likely we are conditioned by cyberattacks, identity theft, computer fraud, and hacking. Unless you understand how to read code and audit algorithms line by line, it is very difficult to relinquish full faith and credit to something that is 100 percent virtual and created by an anonymous character.

This valid apprehension aside, the creation of a new technology whether it be the printing press, the steam engine, or the blockchain does not invalidate its long-term usefulness to society. As Marc Andreessen, famed venture capitalist and founder of Andreessen Horowitz, stated in the *New York Times*:

A mysterious new technology emerges, seemingly out of nowhere, but actually the result of two decades of intense research and development by nearly anonymous researches.

Political idealists project visions of liberation and revolution onto it; establishment elites heap contempt and scorn on it.

On the other hand, technologists—nerds—are transfixed by it. They see within it enormous potential and spend their nights and weekends tinkering with it.

Eventually mainstream products, companies and industries emerge to commercialize it, its effects become profound; and later, many people wonder why its powerful promise wasn't more obvious from the start.

What technology am I talking about? Personal computers in 1975, the internet in 1993, and—I believe— Bitcoin in 2014.[167]

When Satoshi Nakamoto posted his link on a cryptology chat room he wrote: "I've been working on a new electronic cash system that's peer to peer, with no trusted third party." He then posted a link to his white paper. Satoshi went on to describe his creation as "a new electronic cash system that uses a peer-to-peer network to prevent double-spending. It's completely decentralized with no server or central authority."[168]

Naturally, the removal of financial intermediaries would offer substantial cost savings to users. The lack of affiliation with any government or central bank removed the locus of power over money from a central authority and distributed it to all the users, effectively democratizing the control of money. Instead of relying on "trust" in a central authority to appropriately manage the supply of currency, and thereby maintain its value, the Bitcoin ideal aspired to a fixed quantity with a technology, a computer code that determined the way in which new Bitcoins entered the system. Rather than rely on financial institutions to ensure that promises to pay resulted in actual payment, Bitcoin relies on a distributed network of computers (a distributed ledger), linked to each other via the internet to ensure that transactions were legitimate. Each computer linked into the network carries its own copy of the entire history of Bitcoins and Bitcoin transactions, thus when a single transaction occurs, it is not validated by a single financial institution, but instead by the entire network of computers/users/nodes.

Nicholas Mross notes in his documentary The Rise and Rise of Bitcoin that Bitcoin is a "crossroads of technology, philosophy, and economics."[169] Created to offer an alternative to the banking system, Bitcoin is built with mathematical constraints that serve in sharp contrast to modern fiat currency. The finite total possible issuance of twenty-one million Bitcoins harkens back to the gold standard, but without the gold. Some have even dared to call Bitcoin "digital gold."

In his own words, Mross describes the allure of Bitcoin:

Bitcoin is a revolutionary technology that enables a new way to send payments over the internet. You can think of it as an open accounting system, where thousands of open computers all over the world work together to track ownership of digital tokens called Bitcoins. When you send someone a Bitcoin, the transaction is broadcast to the entire network. After it is verified, it's recorded in a public ledger called the blockchain. The blockchain contains a record of every Bitcoin transaction that has occurred since the system began and it's shared and maintained on the network, so everyone keeps the books, so to speak. Most currencies are issued by a central authority that controls the money supply. Bitcoin is a peer-to-peer system, so there is no central authority. Instead, Bitcoins are issued to users who help process transactions in the network. This is known as Bitcoin mining. Bitcoin miners are special computers that do the work required to record transactions in the blockchain. As a reward for their work, the miners are rewarded Bitcoins and this is how new bitcoins get released into circulation. The system is programmed so that only twenty-one million bitcoins will ever exist.[170]

CHAPTER 22

IF BITCOIN WAS THE SPARK, ETHEREUM WAS THE GASOLINE

It is precisely the predestined constraint programmed into Bitcoin that has spurred the subsequent development of myriad other cryptocurrencies, all built on similar technology and catering towards a similar market. The cryptocurrency craze appeared to reach a feverish pitch in late 2017 and early 2018 with an upward surge in cryptocurrency prices and a rush to the market of ICOs or Initial Coin Offerings. For a generation burned by the current traditional financial paradigm and for an increasingly visible libertarian movement seeking maximum freedom from government control and central authority, the digital world of cryptocurrencies presents an alluring alternative.

But how exactly did we get to this point and why? To answer the first part of this question let us examine the work of a twenty-three-year-old college dropout, Vitalik Buterin. In November 2013, Vitalik Buterin wrote the original Ethereum whitepaper, and in July 2015 he launched his company of the same name, declaring, "What Bitcoin does for payments, Ethereum does for anything that can be programmed."[171] Whereas Bitcoin was created with a limited scope in mind—the peer-to-peer processing of payments over the internet via a decentralized network with protections against double payment—Ethereum took blockchain to a whole new level. Described initially as a blockchain app, Ethereum set out to utilize blockchain technology to record "smart contracts" and process transactions and recordkeeping of almost unlimited scale and scope on a decentralized network.

Ethereum is self-described as:

A decentralized platform that runs smart contracts: applications that run exactly as programmed without any possibility of downtime, censorship, fraud or third-party interference.

These apps run on a custom built blockchain, an enormously powerful, shared global infrastructure that can move value around and represent the ownership of property.

This enables developers to create markets, store registries of debts or promises, move funds in accordance with instructions given long in the past (like a will or a futures contract) and many other things that have not been invented yet, all without a middleman or counterparty risk.[172]

So, now that we know what it is, was it successful in its goal?

Can Ethereum Achieve Its Ambitious Goal?

Ethereum's architect Vitalik Buterin is described by George Gilder as "a child prodigy on a Mozartian scale. At four, his favorite toy was an Excel spreadsheet. At seven, he instructed himself in Mandarin and today fluently debates in the language during trips to Shenzhen."[173] He went on to create Ethereum, which, as you will quickly see, has had tremendous success.

Ethereum and the one thousand-plus new company projects on its platform raised "some eight billion dollars in less than one year, exceeding all money raised in IPOs or in venture capital."[174] It was Buterin, the Ethereum team, and his lawyers that created what has become known as the Initial Coin Offering or ICO to raise funds. All of this was made possible by legislation created to help bolster the business community in the wake of the financial crises of 2007–2008. On April 5, 2012, President Barak Obama signed the Jumpstart Our Business Startups Act, which among other things enabled crowdfunding from non-credentialed investors as a new method for business capital raising. Building on the innovation of Bitcoin, Ethereum exploited new legislation to help usher in a flood of similar blockchain-rooted innovations. The significance of Ethereum's contribution to the cryptocurrency movement cannot be overlooked. As Gilder states, "in the history of enterprise there has never been anything like the launch of Ethereum . . . Buterin seems to be on track to exceed Bitcoin and even Satoshi in impact and importance."[175]

Imagine for a moment that Ethereum is successful at achieving its stated goals. Disruption seems too weak a word for the implications to existing commerce. The elimination of "middlemen" and "counterparty risk" would offer both significant efficiency and cost reduction but would similarly wipe out massive sections of the current economy. Imagine purchasing a house and no longer needing to purchase title insurance nor hiring an attorney to conduct a title search and instead relying on the immutable blockchain record, independently maintained on a decentralized network and verified globally. Now imagine the displaced title attorney and the title insurance company. Suddenly, the old phrase "you can't make an omelet without breaking a few eggs" takes on a whole new meaning. In the case of the global economy, "breaking a few eggs" could be more destabilizing than we as a society are prepared to deal with.

Imagine purchasing a house and no longer needing to purchase title insurance nor hiring an attorney to conduct a title search and instead relying on the immutable blockchain record, independently maintained on a decentralized network and verified globally.

I am immediately reminded of a lecture I attended in February 2018. In sunny Las Vegas, X-Prize founder and technology investor Peter Diamandis spoke to a group of the top Financial Advisory Teams in the country at the Barron's Top Advisory Summit. Representing the largest financial firms in the country, literally trillions of investor dollars are managed by the individuals that were in that Aria ballroom. Peter spoke enthusiastically about our technological future. However, halfway through the lecture, the underlying theme of his message began to resonate with everyone in the crowd. Whereas Peter, an investor in disruptive technology, was enthusiastic about the scale in which technology was displacing human effort, the words *efficiency* and *streamlining* were understood to mean the elimination of jobs. The uplifting speech, intended to stimulate excitement about investment opportunities, instead evolved into a dire warning that our industry was on the chopping block and we would all be unemployed in the next decade.

Granted, the alarmist reaction with which the speech was received was an overreaction. After all, this is not the first technological revolution to disrupt the global economy. The agricultural revolution, the industrial revolution, and the computing revolution had similar effects. The problem resides in the speed with which our current technological revolution is occurring and the lack of preparedness workers, governments, school systems, and the economy have in place.

All of this presupposes that blockchain will be successful, a notion that is far from a certainty at this point. Ethereum has agreements with big-name financial institutions such as J.P. Morgan, and Bank of America is rumored to currently hold the most blockchain patents, but these could simply be large financial institutions hedging their bets and business models. In fact, there remain significant concerns within the effectiveness of blockchain, and, within these concerns, Ethereum is also a key player.

CHAPTER 23

THE RISKS OF BLOCKCHAIN, OR HOW CENTRALIZED IS DECENTRALIZED?

Much of the appeal of blockchain and cryptocurrencies is rooted in the decentralized nature of the technology. "The distributed ledger," as the decentralized blockchain network is called, offers users the idea that no one central power or authority can control or alter the network of information. But is this notion of freedom from central authority true?

For technological futurists, the decentralized notion of blockchain and cryptocurrencies offers both a libertarian ideal of how data should be managed as well as a more secure alternative to the current internet architecture, where massive companies such as Google, Amazon, and Facebook have built huge centralized server farms or data centers in which all of the immense data treasure troves of the internet giants are stored. Not only does this internet architecture require intense capital and resource consumption, but it also centralizes the data creating a monopoly of power over it and tempting targets for governments, businesses, and hackers to gain access. In no small way, the centralized nodes of valuable data that constitute the current "cloud" model of digital life carry a dark underbelly of security threats and risks.

The centralized nodes of valuable data that constitute the current "cloud" model of digital life carry a dark underbelly of security threats and risks.

The innovative approach of decentralized blockchain networks made up of millions of distributed computers all over the world working together suggests both a solution to the current security risks as well as a new digital architecture known as "sky computing." Whereas the cloud model concentrates data and activity at choke points (i.e. the clouds themselves), sky computing offers a clear blue sky of millions of decentralized computers without central hubs or chokepoints of risk.

However, in 2017, when the Ethereum blockchain-based company, Distributed Autonomous Corporation, was hacked, some $150 million in the Ethereum cryptocurrency "Ether" was stolen. Ethereum's creator did not stand by idly in the face of this theft. Vitalik Buterin stepped in and entered the Ethereum blockchain code forcibly and reversed the theft. This alteration of the code created what is known as a "hard fork," in which the original code was altered into a new direction and the old code continued on. The result was a split from the original "Ethereum" token to create a rival chain "Ethereum Classic."[176] On the one hand, Buterin's involvement helped right a clear violation and massive theft, but on the other Buterin's power to do so seriously called into question the legitimacy of the proposed benefits of decentralization. Clearly, Buterin exhibited a very centralized authority. Buterin could not resist the urge to intervene, and yet his intervention altered "the immutability of the database and the principle of decentralization that is the heart of the blockchain."[177]

This event created a substantial debate within the blockchain community, but to outsiders and the wider public still evaluating the adoption of the new technology, this event presented a substantial problem. For many people who do not operate within the technology space and have no idea how to code, the notion of immutability within the digital realm is very weak. It is assumed that a clever hacker can change any code or can create a new program that infects a widespread database and alters what was there before it. In other words, the average person simply does not trust code, especially not with their money! The only reason the world sees this level of financial interaction in a digital format is because users know there is a central authority they can turn to if and when things go wrong and seek reparation. The blockchain world, still in its infancy, is too much like the Wild West, and evidence that super hackers with enhanced credentials, such as Buterin, can enter the blockchain to alter the database on a whim is too discomforting. Blockchain expert and author of *The Bitcoin Standard* Saifedean Ammous describes it thus, "The fact that Ethereum could be rolled back means that all blockchains smaller than Bitcoin's are essentially centralized databases under the control of their operators."[178]

Is there a difference between Bitcoin and all of the other blockchains that have followed it? It appears there is. Ethereum and many of the other subsequent blockchains set out to offer enhanced blockchains capable of doing much more than Bitcoin's simple payment objective. Obviously, the intention to offer enhanced capabilities also came with the increased complexity of the code. As scholar and statistician Nassim Taleb stresses in his writings: enhanced complexity leads to enhanced risk. Bitcoin's more streamlined, single-focused objective allowed for a code with a greater focus on security than subsequent followers. As George Gilder puts it, "The key difference between the Bitcoin and Ethereum blockchains is that Bitcoin focuses on security and simplicity while Ethereum focuses on capability and functionality."[179]

Ethereum and the subsequent blockchains are attempting to revolutionize businesses, products, and services.

Ethereum and the subsequent blockchains are attempting to revolutionize businesses, products, and services. Many of these creations are self-described platforms for innovations and interactions that have yet to be invented. Bitcoin, however, was designed to disrupt one thing—money. Disrupting one of the world's oldest technologies is no small task. Bitcoin had to offer characteristics that have been attributed to the most successful examples of money through the ages, not the least of which was security. To do this, Satoshi modeled Bitcoin after the most famous money of all time—gold.

CHAPTER 24

ALL THAT GLITTERS COULD STILL BE GOLD!

s we have discussed in this text, gold has been the dominant form of money and monetary standards throughout much of the human experience. And it is not just the metal itself that has offered the allure. In fact, silver has often supplanted the barbarous relic as the global monetary standard. What then is the primary feature that lends itself to the overwhelming tendency for humans to fall back on these precious metals? Sure, part of the equation is that the metals offer some intrinsic value. However, beyond the commodity value of the metals, there is another characteristic that lends itself to the human mind.

Within the financial markets, there is an ingredient that is at the heart of all research and financial strategy. All economic participants are on a quest for predictability. When uncertainty creeps into the markets, we often see enhanced volatility and both mental and financial strain. As creatures internally programmed to survive on this planet, we crave knowledge to enable us to live another day. Our minds evolved innumerable systems to protect us in an ever-changing environment. Predictability is at the heart of all of our evolutionary advancements. So then, it is without question that in the relatively new financial world we have created for ourselves, we should continue to prize predictability above all other things.

For better or for worse, gold and silver have offered some degree of predictability through the ages. Owing to the relatively low creation of new supplies (the gold supply has grown at roughly 2 percent for centuries) and the capacity of the metals to maintain their integrity over time, gold and silver have offered humans very real predictability.[180] Gold does not tarnish; it does not decay; it does not mix or become diluted with other elements; what is gold today will be gold tomorrow.

The nature of the metals offers predictability, but there has been an overwhelming number of gold- and silver-based coins that have served as money throughout time, only of few of which maintained their value consistently enough for long enough to become famous and remembered today. Several coins minted long ago are still reasonably familiar in the monetary consciousness; the Spanish pieces of eight and the English guinea are two such examples. What sets apart a coin and allows that currency to become a global reserve currency lies within its level of predictability. The Wu Zhu coin in China held its value for five hundred years, while Constantine's Soldarus held its value for seven hundred years.[181] The Spanish pieces of eight and Sir Isaac Newton's English guinea were not imbued with higher quality silver or gold respectively, nor were the designs stamped onto the face of each coin better than others. The resiliency of the coins was in the stability and uniformity with which they were produced over long periods of time. Maintaining a rigid standard of weights and face value and refraining from debasement and revaluing of the coins offered economic participants predictability in an otherwise unpredictable world. The predictability of both the metal and the monetary standard under which the coin was produced solved an important issue facing entrepreneurs and economic participants. They were able to predict through time and space the economic standard of value that their enterprises would produce.

Maintaining a rigid standard of weights and face value and refraining from debasement and revaluing of the coins offered economic participants predictability in an otherwise unpredictable world.

Those raised in an era of fiat currency have little comprehension of how a system of fixed currency would operate. Central banks suggest that targeting a level of predictable inflation fosters a similar stability or predictability, but the reality of our experience tells a different story. To counteract this new paradigm, a multitude of voices call for a return to the gold standard in an effort to tether the monetary base to some fixed and immutable standard. Indeed, China and Russia have been systematically building massive gold reserves as a backstop in the event the world suddenly abandons faith in fiat currency in a disorderly way.

There is, however, substantial economic evidence that life was far from perfect within the gold standard era. It is not certain that either system, as we have known them, is superior to the other. Money by fiat leads to inflation and can substantially destabilize the system over time by fostering debt build-up, as we are currently witnessing within the global economy. The gold standard leads to extreme competition across nations in a never-ending need to maintain gold reserve levels. In the event of economic challenges, the need to protect gold supplies outweighs the needs of the citizens or economic participants, and bad situations can quickly become much worse. Moreover, much of our actual experience with the gold standard also involved bimetallism in which both gold and silver were found in the monetary supply. This, in and of itself, is not necessarily a bad thing. The problem lies in the tendency to declare fixed exchange ratios between the two metals. As discussed earlier within this text, the curious case of fixed exchange rates creates dislocations in value parity causing one of the other metals to disappear from circulation. It is clear to students of economic history that the best method for metal-based reserve systems would likely focus on silver as the primary currency with gold utilized as a reserve, but without a fixed exchange rate between them so that market forces could not disrupt the supply of metals in circulation. But, is reverting back to metals as our monetary base really the answer? Those backing Bitcoin clearly do not think so.

Craving a new answer to the question "what is money?" a generation that was born into the connected world created a digital tool to solve the financial world's shortcomings. Created by hackers operating outside of a central authority, a technological-savvy population moved from the independent ideals of the internet into the realm of independent financial tools. As stated in *The Rise and Rise of Bitcoin*, "Bitcoin is open source software. With open source, the code is publicly available. Anyone can look at it and see how it runs. They can contribute their own changes."[182] It is literally a world in which a wide variety of programmers from around the world cobble together an increasingly improving code that creates the world's first digital attempt at legitimate currency. Creating a world of finite digital tokens that could theoretically serve as a new form of money. This was not too much of a great leap forward for a generation that grew up utilizing digital tokens in video games. In fact, it was a natural extension to the real world of a digital framework already widely used in closed gaming systems.

Craving a new answer to the question "what is money?" a generation that was born into the connected world created a digital tool to solve the financial world's shortcomings.

And the result "is a predictable supply, limited by scarcity. It is somewhat like digital gold. It's the currency of the internet and everyone is free to use it. With Bitcoin you can pay any amount of money to anyone in the world, just as easily as sending an email."[183] The curious rise of a digital replacement for money is timely in an era of fiat money controlled by central banks and a world racked by financial crises. There is without question a rise in calls for a return to metal currency to counteract the consistent printing of new money and the perceived lack of control or predictability afforded to the common user of money. Once again, we can turn to George Gilder to describe the appeal of alternatives to the current monetary paradigm:

> Government monetary systems and financial institutions are foundering. As the economist John Mauldin writes, it's "Code Red" for fiat paper. Gold and commodity markets gyrate portentously. Central Bankers meet solemnly to

decide on levels of "quantitative easing"—on how many trillions of dollars of bonds to buy or sell, thus issuing new money into a flagging economy or sopping up money from a booming one. They hope against hope that these metafictional money fabrications can somehow overflow into the real world of economics and job creation. Lots of luck with that. . . . Meanwhile, somewhere over the rainbow, a possibly mythical man, the pseudonymous Satoshi Nakamoto, invents a new currency called Bitcoin that is spurring a new financial system.[184]

CHAPTER 25

THE BITCOIN
REVOLUTION

The first true monetary use of Bitcoin did not come until 2010 when a Florida man named Laslow Hanyecz offered ten thousand Bitcoins to anyone who would buy him a pizza. A man in London accepted the offer and dialed up Papa John's long distance to purchase Laslow two pizzas, creating what is generally accepted as the first Bitcoin transaction for a tangible good.[185]

However, it was not until late 2010 that Bitcoin had its first real breakthrough as a form of money. When Julian Assange and his organization Wikileaks released thousands of classified US documents, his organization was effectively shut out of the mainstream financial system. Both financial transactions and receipt of donations for the website were terminated by the large banking institutions. Keir Thomas of *PC World* wrote an article on December 10, 2010, titled "Could the Wikileaks Scandal Lead to New Virtual Currency?" where he speculated that donations and funding could be given to the banking quarantined organization through Bitcoin.[186]

Satoshi Nakamoto's last known internet post was in response to that article. Nakamoto said, "It would have been nice to get this attention from any other context. Wikileaks has kicked the hornet's

207

nest, and the swarm is headed towards us."[187] Shortly after that post, Satoshi Nakamoto disappeared. Perhaps he took up a new name online, or perhaps it was never a single person but a group of people like Archimedes could have been. In any event, his creation went on to a larger stage and began to change the world around us. In November 2012, the blogging site WordPress announced it would begin accepting Bitcoin as payment, followed in early 2013 by discussion forum Reddit, which also began accepting Bitcoin.[188] These were the first two widely known websites and corporate service companies to incorporate Bitcoin and signaled the beginning of mainstream acceptance.

Although Bitcoin is in many ways a digital financial revolution, the motto for the revolutionists is far from the rhetoric that made its way around Capitol Hill in 2009 courtesy of Ron Paul chanting "Audit the Fed," or its more aggressive Occupy Wall Street Movement participants shouting "End the Fed." Instead, the crypto movement appears to understand that you are not going to simply end the Fed; rather, "bypass the Fed" is the motto of choice. Perhaps it is the lack of a general effort to tear down current systems that has fostered the slow reactions from regulators and allowed the relatively light approach to constricting cryptocurrency development.

Possibly the most important step in awakening large institutional and high-net-worth investors to the potential value of Bitcoin was not the acceptance of the digital tokens on well-known websites, but a financial calamity on an often-overlooked island. A critical step in global finance unwittingly added fuel to the Bitcoin fire when a financial crisis erupted on a tiny island in the Mediterranean. In response to extreme financial conditions, Cyprus was offered a financial bailout only if they froze and confiscated bank accounts of the citizenry to raise hard cash. Depositors of Cyprus had put their money and their trust into the banks, only to have it taken from them by their government. Strict daily limitations were enacted on a citizen's ability to withdraw cash to purchase basic living supplies. The event vividly illustrated how easily a monetary system with central authorities and chokepoints could appropriate the money of the people.

James Rickards, a former advisor to the CIA, warns in his book *The Road to Ruin* that this is not an isolated risk to a small island nation, but a known tool of governments and much more of a threat than many of us imagine. In his text, he outlines what he calls the Ice-Nine Framework, named after the chemical in Kurt Vonnegut's 1963 book Cat's Cradle, which, when released into water, began a chemical reaction that turned the water into a solid form. Rickards has adopted the nature of Vonnegut's Ice-Nine to reflect government efforts to create a system that allows financial assets to be frozen in the event of a financial crisis. Moving beyond bank closures and bank holidays that citizens witnessed over the last century, Rickards suggests that post-crisis measures such as the Systemically Important Financial Institution (SIFI) system of heightened oversight and regulation have, in fact, allowed the government to essentially freeze brokerage, money market, and other financial securities market assets in the event of a crisis.[189] This suggests that in the event of a crisis, citizens would have substantially more challenging access to capital beyond the bank restrictions faced by the Cypriots.

Suffice to say, the events in Cyprus raised the profile of alternative forms of money immune to such governmental confiscation risks. The big role of cryptocurrency is to separate the government from the control of money and return it to the people. The goal is to "use a currency that is as free as the internet. People crave freedom."[190]

> ## The big role of cryptocurrency is to separate the government from the control of money and return it to the people.

Charlie Shrem, founder of BitInstant, an early cryptocurrency exchange, describes Bitcoin as: "the largest social economic experiment ever conducted in the history of the world . . . Bitcoin is the first product that is digital but also scarce."[191]

Speculative Asset or Global Currency?

But, is Bitcoin, or any of the other cryptocurrencies, actually a currency? Although cryptocurrency has been used by people to make transactions, it has failed widespread adoption in the payment world and has, instead, appeared to most as speculative digital assets more than actual currencies. However, there are those who aim to solve this problem and propel cryptocurrencies forward.

In late 2018, a group of technology entrepreneurs gathered in London, not far from Buckingham Palace, in hopes of reinventing money—again. Bloomberg's Alastair Marsh and Olga Kharif reported on the gathering as follows:

> Call them crypto 2.0. These coins should, as with Bitcoin, allow direct payments between two parties without meddling middlemen or government oversight. Yet, unlike the original cryptocurrency, be stable enough to use in everyday transactions. These recent iterations of digital money, known in the industry parlance as stable coins, are the hottest craze in the world of crypto, with developers from San Francisco

to Seoul racing to get projects to market. While the concept of a low-volatility cryptocurrency has been around since at least 2014, new stable coins are being created at breakneck speed with 120 projects now live or in development.[192]

It is too early to determine if the new generation of cryptocurrencies will truly disrupt or evolve our financial system. Many have compared the current state of cryptocurrencies to the internet in the mid-'90s—clearly, a meaningful technology but exactly how it will change our lives or who the "winners" will be is not yet clear. Cryptocurrency enthusiasts see the entrance of institutional investors into the space as elevating its prestige, with a hope that high-level adoption brings about substantially lower levels of volatility and meaningfully more mature infrastructure.

There is also the question around where the locus of power in defining the role of blockchain and cryptocurrencies will reside globally. To offer a sense of how this plays out, I again turn to the words of the great Niall Ferguson:

A fascinating test of the Chinese approach will be how far they are able to leapfrog ahead of the United States in the rapidly growing sector of financial technology. Of course, the Chinese authorities are no more ready to hand their payments system over to Bitcoin than they are to hand their taxi system over to Uber. Indeed, they are alarmed that 40 percent of the global Bitcoin network is already accounted for by the Chinese "miners," while close to three quarters of Bitcoin trades are on the BTCC (Bitcoin China) exchange. Indeed, regulators effectively shut down the domestic operations of Chinese cryptocurrency exchanges in the summer of 2017. However, Beijing clearly appreciates the potential of blockchain technology. That is why the People's Bank of China and a number of provincial governments are close to launching an "official crytpo-currency"— "Bityuan," perhaps—in one or two provinces in the near future. Singapore may beat Beijing in the race to introduce the first official cryptocurrency, but Beijing will surely beat Washington, D.C. If the Chinese experiments are successful, it would represent the beginning of a new epoch in monetary history, and a serious challenge to the dollar's future as the principal international currency.[193]

As I write this in 2021, we now know that Niall Ferguson was correct and China has successfully introduced the first sovereign cryptocurrency. The question is where will it all go from here? It is without a doubt that blockchain will change our world; we just don't know when, where, or how. Will Bitcoin itself be around to see it? That remains to be seen. At a minimum, the emergence of Bitcoin and the cryptocurrency craze has rejuvenated a centuries-old debate about what is money and who should control it.

The Great Debate

For millennia, humans have debated the role of money in society. In no small part, global society itself seems to have now centered on money as the central organizing principle. Many contend that it is no accident that the population at large has drifted away from the conversation about what is money and who should control it over the past few decades. There are several notable and outspoken personalities—G. Edward Griffin, George Gilder, Murray N. Rothbard, and James Rickards, to name a few—who contend that a group of monetary elites, or monetary scientists, have made every effort to educate the public that a) money is most certainly *not* gold and b) that the science of money is too complex for the average person to comprehend and that the subject should be left to a small minority of specialized participants to guide policy. This notion of complexity exceeding the common person's intellect flies in the face of our history as a civilization. We, the users of money, have long been deeply involved in the monetary conversation with a history of changing the political landscape based on our financial preferences.

We, the users of money, have long been deeply involved in the monetary conversation with a history of changing the political landscape based on our financial preferences.

Within the United States, the debate over money and banking is as old as our nation itself (and indeed older), with Hamilton and Jefferson's debate over central banking an obvious example. As a Tennessean, I immediately think of Andrew Jackson's presidency as a battle against central banks, followed by the 1896 presidential election, in which William Jennings Bryan ran unsuccessfully for the presidency, driven largely by the debate over the role of silver and gold in our monetary system. Beyond the United States, the debate has raged for centuries as the world has continually battled the ultimate question: what is money and who controls it? For the first time in history, the debate has resumed on the global stage with a non-physical item—digital creations known as Bitcoin and cryptocurrencies. In our connected world, linked by instant internet-powered communication, the revolutionary struggle to define money is playing out in real-time on a worldwide scale.

EPILOGUE

I t is my hope that in this text I have presented a brief introduction to the monetary debate. It is no understatement that the inventions of money and central banking have been two of the most important fintech innovations in human history. Although it may be premature to include Blockchain in the same group of world-changing fintech, it certainly appears from these early stages that the monetary debate and power struggle underlying their creation is cut from the same cloth as money and central banking.

Rather than being the end of the debate, Bitcoin and the league of cryptocurrencies it spawned are just another entry in the discussion of what is money and who controls it. In many ways, the rise of Bitcoin is another attempt for the common user of money to obtain some degree of control over the money itself. Our society, no doubt influenced by the series of financial crises that have battered the financial community over recent decades, has become wary of maintaining unwavering trust in the financial central authorities that currently control global money.

As we have seen throughout history, money has the power to unleash both unparalleled social achievement and devastating financial destruction. We have seen how sound money can propel governments and rulers to rise to global dominance. We have also witnessed the slow transmission of financial power from kings and governments to independent central banks and bankers. And we have discussed the efforts made by users of money to anchor the activities of governments and central banks through requirements for inclusion of metal reserves of gold and silver. In many ways, the financial history of humankind is one of a series of revolutions against the tendency for power over money to pool in elite circles.

Bitcoin (and the cryptocurrency explosion) is only the most recent revolutionary attempt to disrupt the centralization of power of money and release it back into the hands of the population. It is similar in nature to the Great Monetary Settlement, as Felix Martin describes the power struggle between the throne of England and the merchant class that resulted in the creation of the Bank of England. The struggle for decentralized power is rooted in other human movements, with democracy being a prime example.

Financial inequality has a disturbing history of creating significant dislocations in social order and is often found at the heart of revolution and war.

It is entirely likely that neither Bitcoin nor any of the known cryptocurrencies are indeed the next evolution of money. They are, however, symbols of a larger struggle. As the world continues down the path of monetary society, there will continue to be inequality in the distribution of resources and power within the system. Financial inequality has a disturbing history of creating significant dislocations in social order and is often found at the heart of revolution and war. We currently live in a world in which financial inequality is at the highest level it has been since the eve of World War I. For many, this is an alarming condition.

Moving the Money Discussion Forward

It is not the purpose of this text to advocate for revolution or a significant change to the current global monetary system. In fact, this book was designed to offer a historical understanding of humankind's long and eventful relationship with money. I hope that I have offered both the benefits and constraints of various financial innovations and strategies. The essential message of this book is that, as of yet, we have not figured out the best system. Until we do, we will continue to experience financial panics, booms, busts, and uncertainty.

It is instead my goal to emphasize our need for a wider swath of our population to continue to study monetary policy with attention to our financial history. It is advisable that we continue to study additional variations of society and social organization itself. For there will be another financial crisis, and as global debt, financial inequality, and diminished financial literacy pile up, the disruption will likely dwarf anything we have seen before. In the absence of widespread research and knowledge of alternative social organization and policy innovations, we, in our moment of highest desperation, run the risk that assertive voices will call for a return to inferior systems.

Rather than moving forward, the pressure of excessive financial strain could easily lead society to take significant steps backward. There is substantially more at stake than global economic growth rates. Indeed, Daron Acemoglu and James Robinson, authors of *Why*

Nations Fail, have pointed out exactly how precious and unlikely the rise of democracy was in England and then what became the United States.[194] Human civilization has had an unfortunate tendency towards concentrated and authoritarian governance. The blooming of democracy and representative government has been an unlikely development for the betterment of human civilization.

Clearly, all forms of government and monetary regimes that we have yet experienced offer advantages and disadvantages. However, the natural state of humankind is innovation. It is important that we continue to explore how to improve upon the progress we have made thus far. This is in no way expected to be easy. Disruption has many enemies, namely those that benefit from the current locus of power and wealth. Perhaps Bitcoin and cryptocurrencies are not the disruptors that will usher in a new era of enhanced human experience, but they are certainly created from that vein. More importantly, they have fostered a new generation of people to give considerable contemplation of money and monetary systems. In my opinion, this renaissance of monetary theory, in and of itself, is their greatest contribution to society.

Disruption has many enemies, namely those that benefit from the current locus of power and wealth.

We have come a long way from Lydia and the creation of money. Policymakers have learned many hard lessons since Swede Johan Palmstruch's days as the world's first central banker. Both money and central banks have gone from disruptive financial technologies to become the two primary underpinnings of our modern monetary society. Central banks, in particular, have both fueled the unprecedented growth of the past three centuries as well as nearly brought the financial system to the brink of collapse a time or two.

Money evolves over time due to frequently occurring revolutions, both big and small. What money is and who controls it are far from fixed propositions. More importantly, in periods in which the nature of money and its locus of control are shifting, there can be substantial disruption to society. We appear to be living through one of those periods now. There is likely a renewed period in which a debate over ideas and monetary technology will define the era. As we have witnessed, the power of money is such that it can propel humanity to new heights and we could be on the verge of a new era of unprecedented prosperity, one in which a greater proportion of the global population is included than ever before. On the other hand, given the complexity of the problems we are collectively facing, the process itself could drive the global economy off a cliff before we find our footing.

Perhaps more alarming is the potential for covert or even explicit financial warfare and the weaponizing of central banks in the pursuit of dominance. Come what may, it is imperative for citizens and market participants alike to understand the significant role central banks have come to play in the marketplace. It is within this paradigm of a resurgence of attention and criticism of central banking that the centuries-old questions of "what is money?" and "who controls it?" have risen back into our social consciousness. The latest fintech developments of Bitcoin, blockchain, and cryptocurrency have emerged as a cyber-punk attempt to redefine and liberate control of money. It remains to be seen how these latest innovations will contribute to or perhaps shift our current global monetary society. To be sure, the discussion is one worth having.

Thank you for your time and attention,
Shaun M. Rowles

A FINAL WORD
FROM THE AUTHOR

If there's one thing I hope you have learned from this book, it's this: *Fintech is always changing.* There is always another revolution on the horizon, and it's our responsibility to participate in these changes as best as we can.

So, despite the daily changes in cryptocurrency and blockchain, the revolutionary case made throughout this book remains valid. But when it comes to *participating* in these changes as best as we can, allow me to leave you with three takeaways.

First, remember that the individual actors and events of a revolution matter less than the actual revolution itself. It's beside the point whether or not Bitcoin, Ethereum, or another technology leads the revolution. The revolution happens anyway.

Second, be aware that the industry changes so rapidly that any deep dive into a new development becomes outdated almost as soon as it's articulated. In other words, we won't find the latest commentary on cryptocurrency or blockchain in this or any book.

Third, if you *are* interested in the day-to-day developments of the current money revolution, I might recommend staying up-to-date by following the experts. For instance, as a financial advisor, it's my role to keep current with trends. That's why, rather than publish my latest findings in a book, I keep my readers updated online with white papers and social media commentary. www.ShaunRowles.com

ENDNOTES

Preface

1 Elgin Groseclose, *Money and Man: A Survey of Monetary Experience* (New York: Frederick Ungar, 1961).

2 Eustace Mullins, *The Federal Reserve Conspiracy* (Union, NJ: Christian Educational Association, 1954).

Introduction

3 John Kenneth Galbraith, *Money: Whence It Came, Where It Went* (Boston: Houghton Mifflin, 1975), 6.

4 Galbraith, *Money: Whence It Came*, 3.

5 Niall Ferguson, *The Ascent of Money: A Financial History of the World*, 10th anniv. ed. (New York: Penguin Books, 2009).

6 George Gilder, *Life after Google: The Fall of Big Data and the Rise of the Blockchain Economy* (Washington, DC: Gateway Editions, 2018), 278.

7 Luke Conway, "Blockchain Explained," Investopedia, June 25, 2019, updated June 1, 2021, https://www.investopedia.com/terms/b/blockchain.asp.

Chapter 2 – A Primer on Human Development

8 Suzana Herculano-Houzel, *The Human Advantage: A New Understanding of How Our Brain Became Remarkable* (Cambridge, MA: MIT Press, 2016).

9 Herculano-Houzel, *Human Advantage*.

10 Charles Fernyhough, *A Thousand Days of Wonder: A Scientist's Chronicle of His Daughter's Developing Mind* (New York: Avery, 2010).

11 Radiolab, "Words with Charles Fernyhough, Susan Schaller, Ann Senghas, James Shapiro, and Elizabeth Spelke," WNYC, August 9, 2010.

12 Radiolab, "Words."

13 Radiolab, "Words."

14 David Graeber, *Debt: The First 5,000 Years* (New York: Melville House, 2011).

15 Niall Ferguson, *The Ascent of Money: A Financial History of the World*, 10th anniv. ed. (New York: Penguin Books, 2009).

16 Graeber, *Debt*, 38.

17 *How Beer Saved the World*, created by Alan Eyres, written by Martyn Ives, aired January 30, 2011, on Discovery Channel.

Chapter 3 – A Brief Introduction into Behavioral Economics

18 Adam Smith, *An Inquiry into the Nature and Causes of the Wealth of Nations* (London: A. Strahan and T. Cadell, 1776).

19 Floris Heukelom, *Behavioral Economics: A History* (New York: Cambridge University Press, 2014), 1.

20 Heukelom, *Behavioral Economics*, 1.

21 George A. Akerlof and Robert J. Shiller, *Animal Spirits: How Human Psychology Drives the Economy, and Why It Matters for Global Capitalism* (Princeton, NJ: Princeton University Press, 2009).

22 John Maynard Keynes, *The General Theory of Employment, Interest, and Money* (London: Macmillan/Palgrave Macmillan, 1936).

23 Walt Kelly, *Pogo*, comic strip, distributed by Post-Hall Syndicate on April 22, 1971. This quote appeared in a daily strip on Earth Day 1971.

24 "We Have Met the Enemy, and They Are Ours," National Park Service, last updated May 24, 2016, https://www.nps.gov/articles/met-the-enemy-4.htm.

Chapter 4 – The Modern Relationship with Money

25 Daniel Kahneman, *Thinking, Fast and Slow* (New York: Farrar, Straus, and Giroux, 2013).

26   Daniel Kahneman and Amos Tversky, "Prospect Theory: An Analysis of Decision under Risk," *Econometrica* 47, no. 2 (March 1979): 263–92, https://doi.org/10.2307/1914185.

27   A. H. Maslow, "A Theory of Human Motivation," *Psychological Review* 50, no. 4 (1943): 370–96, http://citeseerx.ist.psu.edu/viewdoc/download?doi=10.1.1.318.2317&rep=rep1&type=pdf.

28   Dan Ariely and Jeff Kreisler, *Dollars and Sense: How We Misthink Money and How to Spend Smarter* (New York: HarperCollins, 2017).

29   Michelle Singletary, "Your Spending Problem Is All in Your Head—Here's Why," *Washington Post*, November 10, 2017, https://www.washingtonpost.com/business/get-there/your-spending-problem-is-all-in-your-head--heres-why/2017/11/10/22de0f1a-c59a-11e7-84bc-5e285c7f4512_story.html.

30   Xinyue Zhou, Kathleen D. Vohs, and Roy F. Braumeister, "The Symbolic Power of Money: Reminders of Money Alter Social Distress and Physical Pain," *Psychological Science*, Vol 20, pp. 700–706, June 1, 2009.

31   Xinyue Zhou, Kathleen D. Vohs, and Roy F. Braumeister, "The Symbolic Power of Money: Reminders of Money Alter Social Distress and Physical Pain," *Psychological Science*, Vol 20, pp. 700–706, June 1, 2009.

32   Dan Ariely, *Predictably Irrational: The Hidden Forces That Shape Our Decisions* (New York: Harper Perennial, 2010).

33   Ariely, *Predictably Irrational*.

34   John Tierney, "The Advantages of Closing a Few Doors," *New York Times*, February 26, 2008, https://www.nytimes.com/2008/02/26/science/26tier.html.

35   Earnest Calkins, *Business: The Civilizer* (Boston: Little, Brown, 1928).

36   Daron Acemoglu and James A. Robinson, *Why Nations Fail: The Origins of Power, Prosperity, and Poverty* (New York: Currency/Crown, 2013), 384.

Chapter 5 – A Time Before There Were Central Banks

37   "Monetary Policy," Investopedia, reviewed by Thomas Brock, updated December 18, 2020, http://www.investopedia.com/terms/m/monetarypolicy.asp.

38   Milton Friedman, *Money Mischief: Episodes in Monetary History* (New York: Harcourt Brace Jovanovich, 1992).

39   William Henry Furness III, *The Island of Stone Money: Uap of the Carolines* (Philadelphia: J.B. Lippincott, 1910), 95.

40   Furness, *Island of Stone Money*, 96–98.

41   Friedman, *Money Mischief*, 6.

42   Friedman, *Money Mischief*, 10.

43   Elgin Groseclose, *Money and Man: A Survey of Monetary Experience* (New York: Frederick Ungar, 1961).

44   David Graeber, *Debt: The First 5,000 Years* (New York: Melville House, 2011), 24–25.

45   Graeber, *Debt*, 27.

46   Daron Acemoglu and James A. Robinson, *Why Nations Fail: The Origins of Power, Prosperity, and Poverty* (New York: Currency/Crown, 2012).

47   Felix Martin, *Money: The Unauthorized Biography—from Coinage to Cryptocurrencies* (New York: Knopf, 2014).

Chapter 6 – The Birth of Monetary Philosophy

48   Elgin Groseclose, *Money and Man: A Survey of Monetary Experience* (New York: Frederick Ungar, 1961), 9.

49   Jack Weatherford, *The History of Money* (New York: Crown, 1997), 29.

50   Weatherford, *History of Money*, 30.

51   Weatherford, *History of Money*, 30.

52   Weatherford, *History of Money*, 31.

53   Peter L. Bernstein, *The Power of Gold: The History of an Obsession* (Hoboken, NJ: Wiley, 2012), 28.

54   Weatherford, *History of Money*, 32.

55   Felix Martin, *Money: The Unauthorized Biography—from Coinage to Cryptocurrencies* (New York: Knopf, 2014), 76.

56   Martin, *Money: The Unauthorized Biography*, 104.

57   Niall Ferguson, *The Ascent of Money: A Financial History of the World*, 10th anniv. ed. (New York: Penguin Books, 2009).

58   Martin, *Money: The Unauthorized Biography*, 105.

59   Martin, *Money: The Unauthorized Biography*, 83.

60   Martin, *Money: The Unauthorized Biography*, 84.

Chapter 7 – Money: Social Convention or Tool for Sovereign Power?

61   Felix Martin, *Money: The Unauthorized Biography—from Coinage to Cryptocurrencies* (New York: Knopf, 2014), 78.

62   David Graeber, *Debt: The First 5,000 Years* (New York: Melville House, 2011), 298.

63   Martin, *Money: The Unauthorized Biography*, 77.

Chapter 8 – What Shall Be Used as Money and Who Controls It?

64   G. Edward Griffin, *The Creature from Jekyll Island: A Second Look at the Federal Reserve* (Westlake Village, CA: American Media, 2002), 155.

65   Griffin, *Creature from Jekyll Island*, 155–156.

Chapter 9 – From Bullion to Coinage to Banking

66   Peter L. Bernstein, *The Power of Gold: The History of an Obsession* (Hoboken, NJ: Wiley, 2012).

67   Bernstein, *Power of Gold*, 3.

68   Bernstein, *Power of Gold*, 12.

69   Bernstein, *Power of Gold*, 11.

70   Bernstein, *Power of Gold*, 15, 58.

71   *The Rise and Rise of Bitcoin*, directed by Nicholas Mross, written by Patrick Lope, Daniel Mross, and Nicholas Mross (Cleveland, OH: Gravitas Ventures, 2014), documentary.

72   Elgin Groseclose, *Money and Man: A Survey of Monetary Experience* (New York: Frederick Ungar, 1961), 1.

73   Mross, *Rise of Bitcoin.*

74   Murray N. Rothbard, *A History of Money and Banking in the United States: The Colonial Era to World War II* (Auburn, AL: Ludwig Von Mises Institute, 2002), 49.

75   Rothbard, *History of Money and Banking,* 47–48.

76   Felix Martin, *Money: The Unauthorized Biography—from Coinage to Cryptocurrencies* (New York: Knopf, 2014), 100.

77   Martin, *Money: The Unauthorized Biography,* 101.

78   Martin, *Money: The Unauthorized Biography,* 110.

79   Martin, *Money: The Unauthorized Biography,* 110.

80   Carmen M. Reinhart and Kenneth S. Rogoff, *This Time Is Different: Eight Centuries of Financial Folly* (Princeton, NJ: Princeton University Press, 2009), 175.

81   Martin, *Money: The Unauthorized Biography,* 110.

82   Reinhart and Rogoff, *This Time Is Different,* 175.

83   Reinhart and Rogoff, *This Time Is Different,* 179.

84   Niall Ferguson, *The Ascent of Money: A Financial History of the World,* 10th anniv. ed. (New York: Penguin Books, 2009), 66.

85   Martin, *Money: The Unauthorized Biography,* 113.

86   Martin, *Money: The Unauthorized Biography,* 118.

Chapter 10 – The Question of Recoinage and the Vanishing Silver

87   Felix Martin, *Money: The Unauthorized Biography—from Coinage to Cryptocurrencies* (New York: Knopf, 2014), 124.

88   Martin, *Money: The Unauthorized Biography,* 124.

89   Martin, *Money: The Unauthorized Biography,* 125.

90   Martin, *Money: The Unauthorized Biography,* 131.

91   Martin, *Money: The Unauthorized Biography,* 128.

92   Martin, *Money: The Unauthorized Biography,* 128.

93 Martin, *Money: The Unauthorized Biography*, 129.

94 Martin, *Money: The Unauthorized Biography*, 129.

95 Martin, *Money: The Unauthorized Biography*, 130.

96 Peter L. Bernstein, *The Power of Gold: The History of an Obsession* (Hoboken, NJ: Wiley, 2012), 1.

Chapter 11 - The Gold Standard

97 Murray N. Rothbard, *A History of Money and Banking in the United States: The Colonial Era to World War II* (Auburn, AL: Ludwig Von Mises Institute, 2002), 353.

98 Rothbard, *History of Money and Banking*, 354.

99 Peter L. Bernstein, *The Power of Gold: The History of an Obsession* (Hoboken, NJ: Wiley, 2012), 189.

100 Bernstein, *Power of Gold*, 189.

101 Bernstein, *Power of Gold*, 192.

102 Bernstein, *Power of Gold*, 178.

103 George Gilder, *Life after Google: The Fall of Big Data and the Rise of the Blockchain Economy* (Washington, DC: Gateway Editions, 2018), 13.

104 "1661: First Banknotes in Europe," the website for Sveriges Riksbank, https://www.riksbank.se/en-gb/about-the-riksbank/history/historical-timeline/1600-1699/first-banknotes-in-europe/.

105 Liaquat Ahamed, *Lords of Finance: The Bankers Who Broke the World* (New York: Penguin Books, 2009), 12–13.

106 Milton Friedman, *Money Mischief: Episodes in Monetary History* (New York: Harcourt Brace Jovanovich, 1992), 10.

107 Friedman, *Money Mischief*, 11.

108 Elgin Groseclose, *Money and Man: A Survey of Monetary Experience* (New York: Frederick Ungar, 1961).

Chapter 12 – A Brief History of Central Banking

109 Liaquat Ahamed, *Lords of Finance: The Bankers Who Broke the World* (New York: Penguin Books, 2009), 11.

110 Walter Bagehot, *Lombard Street: A Description of the Money Market* (London: Henry S. King, 1873).

111 Bagehot, *Lombard Street*, 57–58.

112 Mohamed A. El-Erian, *The Only Game in Town: Central Banks, Instability, and Avoiding the Next Collapse* (New York: Random House, 2016).

Chapter 13 – The World's First Central Bank

113 "1661: First Banknotes in Europe," the website for Sveriges Riksbank, https://www.riksbank.se/en-gb/about-the-riksbank/history/historical-timeline/1600-1699/first-banknotes-in-europe/.

114 "1661: First Banknotes in Europe," the website for Sveriges Riksbank, https://www.riksbank.se/en-gb/about-the-riksbank/history/historical-timeline/1600-1699/first-banknotes-in-europe/.

115 "1661: First Banknotes in Europe," the website for Sveriges Riksbank, https://www.riksbank.se/en-gb/about-the-riksbank/history/historical-timeline/1600-1699/first-banknotes-in-europe/.

Chapter 14 – The Bank of England

116 "1661: First Banknotes in Europe," the website for Sveriges Riksbank, https://www.riksbank.se/en-gb/about-the-riksbank/history/historical-timeline/1600-1699/first-banknotes-in-europe/.

117 Peter L. Bernstein, *The Power of Gold: The History of an Obsession* (Hoboken, NJ: Wiley, 2012), 181.

118 The website for the Bank of England, https://www.bankofengland.co.uk.

119 Felix Martin, *Money: The Unauthorized Biography—from Coinage to Cryptocurrencies* (New York: Knopf, 2014), 119

120 Martin, *Money: The Unauthorized Biography*, 119.

121 The website for the Bank of England, https://www.bankofengland.co.uk.

Chapter 15 – Money by Fiat

122 James Rickards, *The Road to Ruin: The Global Elites' Secret Plan for the Next Financial Crisis* (New York: Portfolio, 2016).

123 Stacy Schiff, *Cleopatra: A Life* (New York: Little, Brown, 2010), 103.

124 Peter L. Bernstein, *The Power of Gold: The History of an Obsession* (Hoboken, NJ: Wiley, 2012), 173.

125 G. Edward Griffin, *The Creature from Jekyll Island: A Second Look at the Federal Reserve* (Westlake Village, CA: American Media, 2002), 310.

126 Griffin, *Creature from Jekyll Island*, 323.

127 Jerome H. Powell, "America's Central Bank: The History and Structure of the Federal Reserve" (speech), March 28, 2017, West Virginia College of Business and Economics Distinguished Speaker Series, Morgantown, West Virginia, https://www.federalreserve.gov/newsevents/speech/powell20170328a.htm.

128 Neil Irwin, *The Alchemists: Three Central Bankers and a World on Fire* (New York: Penguin Press, 2013), 390.

Chapter 16 – An Introduction to the Federal Reserve

129 Eustace Mullins, *The Federal Reserve Conspiracy* (Union, NJ: Christian Educational Association, 1954).

130 G. Edward Griffin, *The Creature from Jekyll Island: A Second Look at the Federal Reserve* (Westlake Village, CA: American Media, 2002), 155.

131 Danielle DeMartino Booth, *Fed Up: An Insider's Take on Why the Federal Reserve Is Bad for America* (New York: Portfolio, 2017), 42.

132 Booth, *Fed Up*, 42.

133 "Federal Reserve," Wikipedia, last modified May 4, 2021, 21:45, https://en.wikipedia.org/wiki/Federal_Reserve.

134 Booth, *Fed Up*, 42.

Chapter 17 – What Is the Federal Reserve and Where Did It Come From?

135 Roger Lowenstein, *America's Bank: The Epic Struggle to Create the Federal Reserve* (New York: Penguin Press, 2015), 258.

136 Roger T. Johnson, *Historical Beginnings: The Federal Reserve* (Boston: Federal Reserve Bank of Boston, 1990), 8.

137 Johnson, *Historical Beginnings*, 8.

138 Johnson, *Historical Beginnings*, 8.

139 Johnson, *Historical Beginnings*, 9.

140 Johnson, *Historical Beginnings*, 9.

141 Quepeg, "I Killed the Bank," community page for *Daily Kos*, December 7, 2006, https://www.dailykos.com/stories/2006/12/07/278792/-I-killed-the-bank#.

142 Lowenstein, *America's Bank*, 11.

143 Lowenstein, *America's Bank*, 108.

144 Lowenstein, *America's Bank*, 253.

145 "Federal Reserve Bank of Richmond," Federal Reserve History (website), https://www.federalreservehistory.org/time_period?inFields=Time%2520Period:Fed%2527s%2520Formative%2520Years.

146 Woodrow Wilson, "Address after Signing the Currency Bill," (speech), December 23, 1913, Woodrow Wilson Presidential Library & Museum, Staunton, Virginia, https://presidentwilson.org/items/show/29655.

147 Lowenstein, *America's Bank*, 270.

Chapter 18 – Supranational Central Banks

148 Adam LeBor, *Tower of Basel: The Shadowy History of the Secret Bank That Runs the World* (New York: PublicAffairs, 2013), 1.

149 Adam Tooze, *Crashed: How a Decade of Financial Crises Changed the World* (New York: Viking, 2018), 207.

150 Tooze, *Crashed*, 209.

151 Tooze, *Crashed*, 211.

152 Tooze, *Crashed*, 211–212.

153 Tooze, *Crashed*, 214.

154 Tooze, *Crashed*, 214–215.

Chapter 19 – Central Banking Conclusions

155 G. Edward Griffin, *The Creature from Jekyll Island: A Second Look at the Federal Reserve* (Westlake Village, CA: American Media, 2002), 588.

Chapter 20 – The History of Money Revisited

156 *The Rise and Rise of Bitcoin*, directed by Nicholas Mross, written by Patrick Lope, Daniel Mross, and Nicholas Mross (Cleveland, OH: Gravitas Ventures, 2014), documentary.

157 Neal Stephenson, *Cryptonomicon* (New York: Avon Books, 1999).

158 Mross, *Rise of Bitcoin.*

Chapter 21 – Enter Bitcoin

159 Ben Mezrich, *The Accidental Billionaires: The Founding of Facebook—A Tale of Sex, Money, Genius, and Betrayal* (New York: Anchor Books, 2010).

160 Ben Mezrich, "Double Down," *Vanity Fair*, May 2019, https://archive.vanityfair.com/article/2019/5/double-down.

161 George Gilder, *Life after Google: The Fall of Big Data and the Rise of the Blockchain Economy* (Washington, DC: Gateway Editions, 2018).

162 "Satoshi Nakamoto," Wikipedia, last modified June 4, 2021, 4:17, https://en.wikipedia.org/wiki/Satoshi_Nakamoto.

163 Joshua Davis, "The Crypto-Currency: Bitcoin and Its Mysterious Inventor," *New Yorker*, October 3, 2011, https://www.newyorker.com/magazine/2011/10/10/the-crypto-currency.

164 Satoshi Nakamoto, "Bitcoin: A Peer-to-Peer Electronic Cash System," the website for Bitcoin, https://bitcoin.org/bitcoin.pdf.

165 Gilder, *Life after Google*, 119.

166 Gilder, *Life after Google*, 126.

167 Marc Andreessen, "Why Bitcoin Matters," DealBook, *New York Times*, January 21, 2014, https://dealbook.nytimes.com/2014/01/21/why-bitcoin-matters/.

168 Gilder, *Life after Google*, 119.

169 *The Rise and Rise of Bitcoin*, directed by Nicholas Mross, written by Patrick Lope, Daniel Mross, and Nicholas Mross (Cleveland, OH: Gravitas Ventures, 2014), documentary.

170 Mross, *Rise of Bitcoin*.

Chapter 22 – If Bitcoin Was the Spark, Ethereum Was the Gasoline

171 George Gilder, *Life after Google: The Fall of Big Data and the Rise of the Blockchain Economy* (Washington, DC: Gateway Editions, 2018), 111.

172 "Ethereum," the website for Ethereum, https://www.ethereum.org.

173 Gilder, *Life after Google*, 113.

174 Gilder, *Life after Google*, 153.

175 Gilder, *Life after Google*, 153.

Chapter 23 – The Risks of Blockchain, or How Centralized Is Decentralized?

176 George Gilder, *Life after Google: The Fall of Big Data and the Rise of the Blockchain Economy* (Washington, DC: Gateway Editions, 2018), 154.

177 Gilder, *Life after Google*, 154.

178 Saifedean Ammous, *The Bitcoin Standard: The Decentralized Alternative to Central Banking* (Hoboken, NJ: Wiley, 2018).

179 Gilder, *Life after Google*, 154.

Chapter 24 – All That Glitters Could Still Be Gold!

180 George Gilder, *Life after Google: The Fall of Big Data and the Rise of the Blockchain Economy* (Washington, DC: Gateway Editions, 2018), 156.

181 *The Rise and Rise of Bitcoin*, directed by Nicholas Mross, written by Patrick Lope, Daniel Mross, and Nicholas Mross (Cleveland, OH: Gravitas Ventures, 2014), documentary.

182 Mross, *Rise of Bitcoin*.

183 Mross, *Rise of Bitcoin*.

184 Gilder, *Life after Google*, 123.

Chapter 25 – The Blockchain Revolution

185 *The Rise and Rise of Bitcoin*, directed by Nicholas Mross, written by Patrick Lope, Daniel Mross, and Nicholas Mross (Cleveland, OH: Gravitas Ventures, 2014), documentary.

186 Keir Thomas, "Could the Wikileaks Scandal Lead to New Virtual Currency?" *PC World*, December 10, 2010, https://www.pcworld.com/article/213230/could_wikileaks_scandal_lead_to_new_virtual_currency.html.

187 Mross, *Rise of Bitcoin*.

188 Mross, *Rise of Bitcoin*.

189 James Rickards, *The Road to Ruin: The Global Elites' Secret Plan for the Next Financial Crisis* (New York: Portfolio, 2016), 22–24.

190 Mross, *Rise of Bitcoin*.

191 Mross, *Rise of Bitcoin*.

192 Alastair Marsh and Olga Kharif, "Crypto 2.0 May Be Digital Cash You Can Actually Use to Buy Stuff," Bloomberg (website), Bloomberg, LP, updated November 8, 2018, https://www.bloomberg.com/news/articles/2018-11-07/crypto-2-0-may-be-digital-cash-you-can-actually-use-to-buy-stuff.

193 Niall Ferguson, *The Ascent of Money: A Financial History of the World*, 10th anniv. ed. (New York: Penguin Books, 2009), 417–418.

Epilogue

194 Daron Acemoglu and James A. Robinson, *Why Nations Fail: The Origins of Power, Prosperity, and Poverty* (New York: Currency/Crown, 2012).

ABOUT THE AUTHOR

Shaun M. Rowles is an institutional consultant and portfolio manager with two decades of experience and specialization in risk management. He is an author, founder, and guest lecturer in applied macroeconomics at the Vanderbilt University Owen Graduate School of Management. He has a passion for financial history with an emphasis on financial crises and fintech disruptions. An avid conservationist, he's a supporter of socially responsible ESG-themed investing.

He lives in Nashville, Tennessee, with his wife and four children.

> **For more from Shaun, check out: www.ShaunRowles.com**

CPSIA information can be obtained
at www.ICGtesting.com
Printed in the USA
LVHW041334221121
704100LV00004B/64/J